Copyright © 2012 by Abhisek Vyas

Sybase ASE SQL Developer Professional Certification Guide
Version (15.0)

(Exam: C_SASEDP_15)

Published by:
Sybaserays publications

ISBN: 978-1-300-15957-5

First Edition

www.sybaserays.com

All rights reserved. No part of this book may be reproduced or transmitted in any form or by any means, electronic or mechanical, including photocopying, recording, or by any information storage and retrieval system without the written permission of the author, except where permitted by law.

This book has been written with care, neither the author, nor the publisher, nor Sybase Inc are responsible for errors, nor do they accept any liabilities for damages resulting from the use of the information herein.

This book is a work of fiction.

BOOK INTRODUCTION

Acquiring Sybase certifications are becoming a huge task in the field of I.T. More over these exams like *C_SASEDP_15* (previously 510-026) exam are now continuously updating and accepting this challenge is itself a task. This *C_SASEDP_15 (PREVIOUSLY 510-026)* test is an important part of Sybase certifications. We have the resources to prepare you for this. The *C_SASEDP_15 (PREVIOUSLY 510-026)* exam is essential and core part of Sybase certifications and once you clear the exam you will be able to solve the real time problems yourself. Want to take advantage of the Real *C_SASEDP_15 (PREVIOUSLY 510-026)* Test and save time and money while developing your skills to pass your Sybase ASE SQL Developer Professional Exam (Version 15.0) Exam'? Let us help you climb that ladder of success and pass your *C_SASEDP_15 (PREVIOUSLY 510-026)* now!

You will find inside:
- **More than 400 questions and answers.**
- **120 Important demo questions.**
- **100 % guranteed pass.**

Acquiring Sybase certifications are becoming a huge task in the field of I.T. More over these exams like *C_SASEDP_15 (PREVIOUSLY 510-026)* exam are now continuously updating and accepting this challenge is itself a task. This *C_SASEDP_15 (PREVIOUSLY 510-026)* test is an important part of Sybase certifications. We have the resources to prepare you for this. The *C_SASEDP_15 (PREVIOUSLY 510-026)* exam is essential and core part of Sybase certifications and once you clear the exam you will be able to solve the real time problems yourself. Want to take advantage of the Real *C_SASEDP_15 (PREVIOUSLY 510-026)* Test and save time and money while developing your skills to pass your Sybase ASE SQL Developer Professional Exam (Version 15.0) Exam'? Let us help you climb that ladder of success and pass your *C_SASEDP_15 (PREVIOUSLY 510-026)* now!

C_SASEDP_15 (PREVIOUSLY 510-026) questions and answers, updated regularly
Verified *C_SASEDP_15 (PREVIOUSLY 510-026)* answers by Experts and bear almost 100% accuracy
C_SASEDP_15 (PREVIOUSLY 510-026) tested and verified before publishing
C_SASEDP_15 (PREVIOUSLY 510-026) same questions as real exam with multiple choice options

Guaranteed Results
One of the best and most rewarding features of the *C_SASEDP_15 (PREVIOUSLY 510-026)* training materials are garanteed to bring you success in the testing room. Pass with total confidence.

ABOUT AUTHOR

- Sybase certified professional.
- Database consultant with more than 8 years of experience in international industry.
- Worked for various industy projects.
- Dept knowledge on Investing Banking Projects.
- Working as a database consultant for Dell services (Singapore).

Personal Detail:

Name: Abhisek Vyas
WWW: www.sybaserays.com
Email: abhiboss25@gmail.com

If you want to contact me, Please contact me via email.

Sybase ASE SQL Developer Professional Exam (Version 15.0)

Section 1 - What's New in ASE 15 (9 questions - 15%) 6
    1.1   Describe local/global indexes on partitioned tables 6
    1.2   Identify aspects of insensitive/semi-sensitive scrollable cursors 7
    1.3   Describe metrics capture 9
    1.4   Identify and define new commands for getting optimizer information 11
    1.5   Describe ASE 15.0 optimization goals and their impact on query plans 12
    1.6   Describe the various join types (hash joins, merge joins, NLJ, N-ary NLJ) 13

Section 2 - ASE Performance and Tuning Basics (2 questions - 4%) 14
    2.1   Define tradeoffs of performance & tuning - with an emphasis on code 14
    2.2   Identify steps involved in executing a query 15
    2.3   List what query plan information can be viewed 16

Section 3 - Logical and Physical Design (2 questions - 4%) 17
    3.1   Define Entities, Relationships (subtype-supertype) & Attribute cardinality 17
    3.2   Assess a relational data model 17
    3.3   Create Associative Tables 17
    3.4   Identify qualities for Primary Key 17
    3.5   Represent relationships as Foreign keys 18
    3.6   Determine column data type and null/not null status, default values, rules & constraints 19
    3.7   Define derived tables, intra-row derived columns and inter-row derived columns 19
    3.8   List advantages of normalization 20
    3.9   Understand First, Second and Third Normal Form 21
    3.10   List denormalization techniques 21

Section 4 - ANSI SQL – DDL (5 questions – 8 %) 22
    4.1   Describe how to create tables, views, indexes, etc. 22
    4.2   Define column properties such as null and identity 23
    4.3   Define temporary tables 24
    4.4   Describe ASE data types 25
    4.5   Describe different partitioning strategies 25
    4.6   Understand partitioning options with alter table 28

Section 5 - ANSI SQL - DML (5 questions – 8 %) 29
    5.1   Describe the data manipulation commands: select, insert, update, and delete, and the use of cursors 29
    5.2   Identify important clauses of DML statements, such as where, having, order by, etc. 35
    5.3   Identify the performance and tuning aspects of DML statements, such as direct and deferred updates, etc. 36
    5.4   Identify techniques to promote the most efficient update method 38
    5.5   Understand computed columns: 39

Section 6 - Query Access Methods (5 questions – 8 %) 40
    6.1   Define range queries, point queries, and covered queries 41

6.2	Explain how ASE accesses data in selects, inserts, deletes, and updates	42
6.3	Define I/O for a select using a non-clustered index	43
6.4	Define performance benefits of using indexes	44
6.5	Define logging & minimally-logged operations	44

Section 7 - Query Optimization (9 questions – 15 %) 45

7.1	Define the 'Or Strategy' and showplan, plus options	45
7.2	Identify optimization 'set' command tools	47
7.3	Use of Abstract Plans	49
7.4	Determine if the optimizer selected serial or parallel access	52
7.5	Define Procedure Cache & explain how stored procedures are processed	55
7.6	Identify factors for setting Prefetch at the Query-Level	56
7.7	Identify Query Degradation	56
7.8	Identify tasks for which internal working tables are created in tempdb or in memory	57
7.9	Design queries to take maximum advantage of optimizer features	57
7.10	Describe how the optimizer analyzes search arguments (SARG)	57
7.11	Identify factors of Subquery Optimization	57

Section 8 - Stored Procedures and Triggers (4 questions – 6 %) 58

8.1	Write and tune stored procedures and triggers	58
8.2	Define query plans and the procedure cache	60
8.3	Define triggers and their usage	61

Section 9 - Transact-SQL Statements (5 questions – 8 %) 62

9.1	Use of Sybase-specific Transact-SQL commands, such as functions, programming commands such as if and while, local and global variables	63
9.2	Describe 'scrollable cursors'	64
9.3	Identify guidelines for SARGs	64
10.2	Describe traditional Sybase data integrity mechanisms such as rules and defaults	67

Section 11 - Transaction Management and Locking (5 questions – 8 %) 67

11.1	Describe the behavior of transactions and transaction management commands	67
11.2	Describe behavior of locks	69
11.3	Describe transaction logging; lock blocking, diagnosis and resolution of deadlocks [PnT-Locking]	72
11.4	Describe the effect of transaction isolation levels	72
11.5	Define methods for reducing lock contention	74
11.6	Describe how ASE resolves a deadlock	74

Section 12 - Joins, Subqueries, and Unions (4 questions – 6 %) 74

12.1	Define the different types of joins	74
12.2	Describe the union and union all command	75
12.3	Describe subqueries	75

Section 13 - Optimizer Statistics (3 questions – 6 %) 76

13.1   Describe table-level and distribution statistics 76
13.2   Define the different types of statistics, such as cluster ratios, density values, and histograms 77
13.3   Describe simulated statistics 79
IMPORTANT: DEMP QUESTION PAPER 80

Certification: C_SASEDP_15

Section 1 - What's New in ASE 15 (9 questions - 15%)

1.1 Describe local/global indexes on partitioned tables

1. Global indexes can be clustered on
   A. Round robin partitioned tables only.
   B. Round robin or range partitioned tables.
   C. Round robin, range or hash partitioned tables.
   D. List partitioned tables only.

Answer: A

2. What conditions must be met before altering the partition strategy of a table from round-robin to a range partitioned table?
   A. Additional partitions must be added to the round-robin table
   B. Table must be un-partitioned before changing partition strategy
   C. Table data must be truncated
   D. Table indexes must be dropped

Answer: D

3. Which of the following statements is NOT true?
   A. A partitioned table can have partitioned and unpartitioned indexes.
   B. An unpartitioned table can have only unpartitioned, global indexes.
   C. All unpartitioned indexes on unpartitioned tables are global.
   D. local index spans all data partitions in a table.

Answer: D

4. Which of the following statements is NOT true?
   A. Local indexes can increase concurrency through multiple index access points
   B. You can place local nonclustered index subtrees (index partitions) on separate segments to increase I/O parallelism.
   C. You can not run reorg rebuild on a per-partition basis
   D. Global nonclustered indexes are better for covered scans than local indexes

Answer: C

5. Global, nonclustered, unpartitioned indexes can be created on
   A. Round robin partitioned tables
   B. Range and Hash partitioned tables
   C. List partitioned tables
   D. All of the above

Answer: D

6. If you run following statement on partitioned table
   create nonclustered index ord_idx on mysalesdetail (au_id)
   It will create
   A. global clustered index
   B. global nonclustered index

C. local clustered index
D. local non clustered index

Answer: B

7. A local index inherits from the base table
   A. partition types
   B. partitioning columns
   C. partition bounds
   D. All of the above

Answer: D

8. Which of the following statement is NOT true [Choose 2]?
   A. You can create global indexes that are nonclustered and unpartitioned for all partitioning table strategies.
   B. The index and the data partitions can NOT reside on the different segments.
   C. You can NOT create the index on any indexable column in the table.
   D. All of the above

Answer: B, C

9. Which of the following is FALSE about local index?
   A. It requires a separate index structure for each data partition.
   B. It may be clustered or nonclustered.
   C. In a clustered local index, data is sorted separately within each partition.
   D. Clustered local indexes are allowed on a round robin table with more than one partition.

Answer: D

10. Which of the following is NOT TRUE about function based indexes?
    A. All inserts, updates and deletes cause updates to the function-based index.
    B. Queries only recognize the index if the expression is identical to the one used in the index.
    C. Function based indexes are helpful for DSS queries and user-defined sorting.
    D. Function based indexes can be created with the "sorted_data" option.

Answer: D

1.2 Identify aspects of insensitive/semi-sensitive scrollable cursors

11. Scrollable Cursor can NOT be
    A. semi-sensitive
    B. insensitive
    C. sensitive
    D. None of the above

Answer: C

12. Which of the following statement is NOT true?
    A. For scrollable cursors in ASE 15, the only valid cursor specifica- tion is "for read only."
    B. All update cursors are scrollable.
    C. Non-scrollable, insensitive cursors are also supported on Open Server and are set with the **CS_NOSCROLL_INSENSITIVE** option
    D. A scrollable cursor allows you to set the position of the cursor anywhere in the cursor result set

Answer: B

13. Which of the following are correct about insensitive cursors? (Choose 2)
    A. The data set can become stale.
    B. Locks cannot be released even after the completion of the work table.
    C. Changes to the base tables are not seen by the cursor.
    D. Waiting may be required to find the next row.
Answer: A, C

14. Which of the following are TRUE about the cursor fetch statement? (Choose 2)
    A. The row number starts at 0.
    B. If fetch behavior is not specified, the next row is assumed by default.
    C. For a scrollable cursor, @@rowcount cannot exceed the total number of rows in the result set.
    D. @@fetch_status=0 implies the last fetch was successful.
Answer: B, D

15. Which option is not correct for scrollable cursor?
    A. First
    B. Next
    C. previous
    D. relative
Answer: C (prior -- fetch the previous row in the cursor result set.)

16. Which of the following statement is NOT correct?
    A. The default cursor_scrollability is no scroll.
    B. The default cursor_sensitivity is insensitive.
    C. No support for the concept of "sensitive" exists in ASE 15.
    D. cursor_scrollability can be defined as scroll or no scroll.
Answer: B (The default for the cursor is semi-sensitive.)

17. Which of the following statement is NOT correct?
    A. The insensitive cursor shows only the result set as it is when the cursor is opened.
    B. Data changes in the underlying tables are visible to insensitive cursor.
    C. Some changes in the base tables made since opening the cursor may appear in the result set.
    D. Data changes may or may not be visible to the semi-sensitive cursor.
Answer: B (data changes in the underlying tables are not visible to insensitive cursor)

18. Which of the following statement is TRUE about insensitive cursor [Choose 2]?
    A. When you declare and open an insensitive cursor, a worktable is created and fully populated with the cursor result set.
    B. Locks on the base table are NOT released.
    C. only the worktable is used for fetching.
    D. only the base table is used for fetching.
Answer: A, C

19. Which of the statement is TRUE if you run following commands (if isolation level is 1.)
declare CurSr_SS semi_sensitive scroll cursor for
select emp_id, fname, lname
from emp_tab
where emp_id > 2002000

open CurSr_SS
fetch last CurSr_SS
    A. All the qualified rows of the cursor CurSr_SS will be copied to the worktable.
    B. Locking on the base table, *emp_tab*, will not be released.
    C. The result set of cursor CurSr_SS is fixed.
    D. None of the above.
Answer: A, C

20. Cursor sensitivity...
    A. disables the scrollability function.
    B. controls when the work table is built.
    C. allows users to fetch rows by position.
    D. forces a table scan to generate the result set.
Answer: B

21. Semi-sensitive scrollable cursors can... (Choose 2)
    A. fetch any specific row of the work table.
    B. fetch any row relative to the current cursor position.
    C. update any row of the work table.
    D. delete any row of the work table.
Answer: A, B

22. Which of the following are fetch restrictions for a scrollable cursor? (Choose 3)
    A. Row numbers start at 1, not 0.
    B. Negative values of fetch_offset move backwards.
    C. Row numbers start at 0, not 1.
    D. If the fetch_offset positions the cursor beyond the last row or before the first row, no data is returned and no error is raised.
    E. Negative values are not used in scrollable cursors.
Answer: A, B, D

1.3 Describe metrics capture

23. Which of the following Query Processing Metric don't have **minimum**, **maximum**, and **average** values? [Choose 2]
    A. CPU execution time
    B. Count
    C. Abort count
    D. Elapsed time
Answer: B, C

24. Which of the following statement is NOT true?
    A. You can not use QP metrics at the server level.
    B. You can activate and use QP metrics at the session level.
    C. The QP metrics for ad hoc statements are captured directly into a system catalog
    D. QP metrics for statements in a stored procedure are saved in a procedure cache.
Answer: A

25. Which of the following command is correct to enable QP metrics at session level?

A. sp_configure "enable metrics capture", 1
B. set metrics_capture on/off
C. set query_metrics_capture on/off
D. None of the above

Answer: B

26. Which are the following configuration parameters that set the query metrics threshold for capture into the catalog?
A. metrics elap max
B. metrics exec max
C. metrics pio max
D. metrics lio max
E. All of the above

Answer: E

27. Which of the following statement is NOT true about **sp_metrics**?
A. Adaptive Server using sp_metrics to manage sysquerymetrics data.
B. The data most currently collected is stored in sysquerymetrics with a global ID (GID) of 1.
C. To find the next available GID, select the min(gid) from sysquerymetrics and add one to the value.
D. Backs up, drops, and flushes QP metrics.

Answer: C (the next available GID, select the **max(gid)** from sysquerymetrics and add one to the value.)

28. Which of the following statistics are NOT captured by QP Metrics?
A. Elapsed time
B. Logical I/O
C. Physical I/O
D. Subquery caching

Answer: D

29. Metrics capture gives the administrator the ability to see which query performed (Choose 2)
A. The most physical I/O.
B. The least logical I/O.
C. A table scan.
D. A clustered index scan.
E. Large I/O.

Answer: A, B

30. QP Metrics allow a user to capture the (Choose 2)
A. Indexes chosen by the optimizer.
B. Table join order.
C. Cpu execution time.
D. Number of logical I/O used.
E. Number of rows returned.
F. Number of worktables used.

Answer: C, D

31. Which of the following statement is NOT true about the QP Metrics capture process?
- Enabled at the server level with the sp_configure parameter
- Can be used to identify the query with the most physical I/O.
- Captures server-wide data to a centralized table in the master database from all user databases

- Can be used to identify the most frequently executed query in a database
- None of the above

Answer: C

1.4 Identify and define new commands for getting optimizer information

32. What is used to determine how many rows qualify for the search argument?
    A. Histogram
    B. Forwarded rows
    C. Data cluster ratio
    D. Index cluster ratio

Answer: A

33. Which function measures the amount of change in the data distribution since update statistics?
    A. data_pages
    B. count
    C. datachange
    D. used_pgs

Answer: C

34. **Datachange() function** is the key to identifying whether **update statistics** operations is necessary on a
    A. Table
    B. Index
    C. Partition
    D. Column
    E. All of the above

Answer: E

35. datachange is reset or initialized to zero when
    A. New columns are added, and their datachange value is initialized.
    B. New partitions are added, and their datachange value is initialized.
    C. Data is truncated for a table or partition, and its datachange value is reset.
    D. Data-partition-specific histograms are created, deleted or updated. When this occurs, the datachange value of the histograms is reset for the corresponding column and partition
    E. A table is repartitioned either directly or indirectly as a result of some other command, and the datachange value is reset for all the table's partitions and columns.
    F. A table is unpartitioned, and the datachange value is reset for all columns for the table.
    G. All of the above

Answer: G

36. Which of the following statement is NOT true about **datachange** function?
    A. datachange is a measure of the inserts, deletes and updates but it does not count them individually.
    B. The value that datachange displays is the in-memory value.
    C. The datachange values is reset when histograms are created for global indexes on partitioned tables.
    D. Instead of consuming resources, datachange discards the descriptor for an object that is not already in the cache.

Answer: C

37. Which of the following statement is true about **datachange** function [Choose 2]?
    A. datachange statistics can be maintained on tables in system tempdbs, user-defined tempdbs, system tables, or proxy tables.
    B. datachange updates are transactional.
    C. If memory allocation for column-level counters fails, Adaptive Server tracks partition-level datachange values instead of column-level values.
    D. If Adaptive Server does not maintain column-level datachange values, it then resets the partition-level datachange values whenever the datachange values for a column are reset.
Answer: C, D

38. Which set command shows the details of useful statistics missing from SARG/Join columns.
    A. set statistics plancost
    B. set option show_missing_stats
    C. set option show_best_plan
    D. set option show_search_engine
Answer: B

39. How can you detect if a query is missing statistics useful for optimization?
    A. Query systatistics and systabstats after running the query
    B. Run update statistics before running the query
    C. Query monProcessActivity after running the query
    D. Run set option show_missing_stats before running the query
Answer: D

40. Which statements are TRUE about the 'newid()' built-in function?
    A. The newid() function can be initialized with a seed value.
    B. The newid() function can generate a 16-byte value.
    C. The values generated are guaranteed to be unique inside the database.
    D. The values generated by newid() are guaranteed to be unique inside the server.
Answer: D

41. A server level configuration parameter, "sproc optimize timeout limit", is used to control the optimizer timeout limit when compiling stored procedure queries. What is the default value?
    A. 0
    B. 1
    C. 10
    D. 40
Answer: D

42. Which of the following is TRUE about the optimization timeout limit configuration parameter?
    A. timeout value can only be specified at the server level.
    B. Timeout values apply to both ad-hoc queries and stored procedures.
    C. Higher timeout values are used for faster compilation time.
    D. Timeout value represents the percent (%) of estimated query execution time.
Answer: D

1.5 Describe ASE 15.0 optimization goals and their impact on query plans

43. If a query should use Nested Loop Joins, what optimization goal setting is recommended?
    A. None, use the default
    B. allrows_mix

C. allrows_oltp
D. allrows_dss

Answer: C

44. The allrows_oltp optimization goal considers
    A. Bushy trees.
    B. Hash joins.
    C. Merge joins.
    D. Nested loop joins.
    E. Parallelism.
    F. All optimization methods.

Answer: D

45. Optimization goals can not be apply at
    A. session level
    B. procedure level
    C. server level
    D. query level

Answer: B

46. Given the following query :
SET showplan, noexec on
GO
SELECT * from authors a, titleauthor ta, titles t where ta.au_id=a.au_id and ta.title_id=t.title_id
Which statement SHOULD be appended to enable hash join?
    A. plan (use optgoal allrows_dss)
    B. plan (use optgoal allrows_oltp)
    C. plan (use optgoal allrows_mix)
    D. set optgoal allrows_mix

Answer: A

1.6 Describe the various join types (hash joins, merge joins, NLJ, N-ary NLJ)

47. In version earlier than 15.0, which join strategy was the primary JOIN strategy?
    A. MERGE JOIN
    B. HASH JOIN
    C. NESTED LOOP JOIN
    D. NARY NESTED LOOP JOIN

Answer: C

48. Which strategy is effective when there is a useful index available for qualifying the join predicates on the inner stream?
    A. MERGE JOIN
    B. HASH JOIN
    C. NESTED LOOP JOIN
    D. NARY NESTED LOOP

Answer: C

49. Which strategy is effective when a scan of the data streams requires that most of the rows must be processed, and that, if any of the input streams are large, they are already sorted on the join keys?

A. MERGE JOIN
B. HASH JOIN
C. NESTED LOOP JOIN
D. NARY NESTED LOOP

Answer: A

50. Which strategy is good in cases where most of the rows from the source sets must be processed and there are no inherent useful orderings on the join keys?
    A. MERGE JOIN
    B. HASH JOIN
    C. NESTED LOOP JOIN
    D. NARY NESTED LOOP

Answer: B

51. The input row width in HASH join limited to?
    A. 32 kilobytes
    B. 10 kilobytes
    C. 64 kilobytes
    D. 100 kilobytes

Answer: C

52. An N-ary join is (Choose 2)
    A. A type of hash join.
    B. A type of nested loop join.
    C. A type of sort merge join.
    D. An optimization for joins of tables with no qualifying join indexes.
    E. An optimization for joins of three or more tables.

Answer: B, E

53. Which type of merge join does not require a sort of the data to occur?
    A. sort-merge
    B. left-merge
    C. right-merge
    D. full-merge

Answer: D

Section 2 - ASE Performance and Tuning Basics (2 questions - 4%)

2.1 Define tradeoffs of performance & tuning - with an emphasis on code

54. When you execute sp_configure to modify a dynamic parameter:
    A. The configuration and run values are updated.
    B. The configuration file is updated.
    C. The change takes effect immediately.
    D. All of the above

Answer: D

55. When you execute sp_configure to modify a static parameter:
    A. The configuration value is updated.
    B. The configuration file is updated.
    C. The change takes effect only when you restart Adaptive Server.
    D. All of the above
Answer: D

56. In sp_configure command, each configuration parameter has an associated display level and default is
    A. basic
    B. intermediate
    C. comprehensive
    D. None of the above
Answer: C

57. Which of the following statements are true about MDA tables (Choose 3)?
    A. MDA tables can be accessed with regular SQL select statements
    B. The MDA tables report information about ASE at a high level.
    C. MDA tables report data at the query and table level in addition to the server level.
    D. MDA tables provide information on current activity at the table, procedure, query, and process levels.
Answer: A, C, D (The MDA tables report information about ASE at a low level.)

58. Provides statistics about process activity
    A. monProcessWorkerThread
    B. monProcessObject
    C. monProcess
    D. monProcessActivity
Answer: D

59. Provides the SQL text that is currently being executed.
    A. monSysSQLText
    B. monSysStatement
    C. monProcessSQLText
    D. monSysPlanText
Answer: C

60. Which is the correct command to print only Data Cache Management section report by sp_sysmon?
    A. sp_sysmon "00:05:00", dcache
    B. sp_sysmon "00:05:00"
    C. sp_sysmon "00:05:00","dataManagement"
    D. sp_sysmon 05, dcache
Answer: A

2.2 Identify steps involved in executing a query

61. The parser converts the text of the SQL statement to an internal representation called a
    A. Query plan
    B. Query text

C. Query tree
D. Query sql
Answer: C

62. In which order query processor access query processor modules?
    A. parser, normalization, optimizer, preprocessor, code generator, procedural execution engine, query execution engine
    B. parser, optimizer, preprocessor, normalization, code generator, procedural execution engine, query execution engine
    C. parser, normalization, preprocessor, optimizer, code generator, procedural execution engine, query execution engine
    D. parser, preprocessor, normalization, optimizer, code generator, query execution engine, procedural execution engine
Answer: C

63. Which of the statement is NOT correct about parallelism in ASE 15?
    A. Vertical parallelism provides the ability to use multiple CPUs at the same time.
    B. Horizontal parallelism allows the query to access different data located on different partitions at same time.
    C. ASE handles both horizontal and vertical parallelism.
    D. Horizontal parallelism allows the query to access different data located on different disk devices at same time.
    E. None of the above
Answer: E

2.3 List what query plan information can be viewed

64. To see query plans, use:
    A. set queryplan on
    B. set displayplan 1
    C. set showplan on
    D. set displayplan on
Answer: C

65. Which of the following statements are TRUE in reference to the output of showplan display? (Choose 3)
    A. Query plans describe the order of execution from a top-down perspective.
    B. Query plans can be composed from over thirty different operators.
    C. Query plans are upside down trees of Operators.
    D. Query plans display sub-plans that are executed in parallel.
    E. Query plans show the three best plans of parallel query execution.
Answer: B, C, D

66. Where are QP Metrics stored?
    A. sysqueryplans
    B. sysquerymetrics
    C. syscomments
    D. monProcessSQLText
    E. monStatement
Answer: A

Note: sysquerymetrics is a view not a table. This view is comprised of two instances of the sysqueryplans table from within the same database, joined via a self join.

Section 3 - Logical and Physical Design (2 questions - 4%)

3.1 Define Entities, Relationships (subtype-supertype) & Attribute cardinality

67. There are three kinds of relationships between tables. Those are [Choose 3]
    A. One-to-one
    B. One-to-many
    C. Many-to-many
    D. Many-to-one

Answer: A,B,C

3.2 Assess a relational data model

68. Which of the following rules are not true about a relation in RDBMS? [Choose 2]
    A. Relation (file, table) is a two-dimensional table.
    B. Attribute (i.e. field or data item) is a column in the table.
    C. Each column in the table has a unique name within that table.
    D. Each column is not homogeneous.
    E. The order of the rows and columns is important.

Answer: D, E

69. Surrogate key or artificial key is used as a primary key when... (Choose 2)
    A. none of the candidate keys satisfy all the criteria for a primary key.
    B. natural key exist but it is too large or complex.
    C. some of the candidate keys satisfy all the criteria for a primary key.
    D. natural key exist and it is less that 25 bytes.

Answer: A, B

3.3 Create Associative Tables

70. Associative entities are also referred to as?
    A. Supporting entities
    B. Resolving entities
    C. Create entities
    D. None of the above

Answer: B

3.4 Identify qualities for Primary Key

71. Which of statements are NOT true about primary key? [Choose 2]
    A. Each table in a relational database must have a primary key

B. The primary key can a column or set of columns
C. No two rows may have the same value of a primary key
D. Default type of Primary is a type of **non clustered** type of index
E. If you drop a table, associate primary key will be dropped automatically

Answer: A, D

72. Which of the following structures can be used to enforce entity integrity? (Choose 2)
    A. Trigger
    B. sp_primarykey
    C. Check constraint
    D. References constraint
    E. Primary key constraint

Answer: A, E

73. Which of the method is not correct for creating a primary key?
    A. CREATE TABLE employee
        (emp_id int PRIMARY KEY ,
        emp_name char(50),
        emp_addess varchar(255))
    B. CREATE TABLE employee
        emp_id int CONSTRAINT pk_emp_id PRIMARY KEY ,
        emp_name char(50),
        emp_addess varchar(255))
    C. CREATE TABLE employee
        (emp_id int ,
        emp_name char(50),
        emp_addess varchar(255),
        CONSTRAINT pk_emp_id PRIMARY KEY (emp_id)
)
    D. None of the Above

Answer: D

3.5 Represent relationships as Foreign keys

74. A **Foreign key** is a field (or fields) that points to the _____ of another table.
    A. Foreign key
    B. Primary Key
    C. Unique key
    D. No key

Answer: B

75. The purpose of the foreign key is to ensure
    A. entity integrity
    B. domain integrity
    C. referential integrity
    D. check integrity

Answer: C

76. Creating an index on a foreign key is often useful for the following reasons [Choose 2]
    A. Changes to PRIMARY KEY constraints are checked with FOREIGN KEY constraints in related tables.
    B. An index disables the Database Engine to quickly find related data in the foreign key table.
    C. A FOREIGN KEY constraint can reference columns in tables in the same database or within the same table.
    D. None of the above
Answer: A, C

3.6 Determine column data type and null/not null status, default values, rules & constraints

77. The DEFAULT constraint is used to insert a
    A. a default value into a table
    B. a 0 value into a column
    C. a default value into a column
    D. NULL value into a column
Answer: C

78. Which are the statements are true about default constraints? [Choose 3]
    A. You can include only one default clause per column in a table.
    B. You can bind a new default to a datatype without unbinding the old one.
    C. The new default do not overrides and unbinds the old one.
    D. You can not bind a new default to a datatype without unbinding the old one.
    E. You must unbind a default with sp_unbindefault, before you drop it otherwise it will give error.
Answer: A, B, E

79. Which statements are TRUE. Defaults & rules... (Choose 2)
    A. can implement multi column checks.
    B. can be associated with user defined data types.
    C. can have associated messages.
    D. are not created when a table is created.
Answer: B, D

3.7 Define derived tables, intra-row derived columns and inter-row derived columns

80. Which of the statement are true for derived table?
    A. Derived table is defined by the evaluation of a query expression.
    B. It is not different from a regular table.
    C. Derived table is not defined by the evaluation of a query expression
    D. It is different from a regular table.
Answer: A, D

81. Derived table described in
    A. system catalogs
    B. user catalogs
    C. stored on disk

D. None of the above.
Answer: D

82. A derived table may be a [Choose 2]
    A. a permanent user table
    B. a SQL derived table
    C. an abstract plan derived table
    D a system table
Answer: B, C

83. Which of the statements are true about SQL derived tables? [Choose 2]
    A. The SQL derived table persists only for the duration of the query.
    B. A SQL derived table used multiple times performs comparably to a query using a view with a cached definition.
    C. The SQL derived table persists for entire session.
    D. We need to drop SQL derived tables
Answer: A, B

84. Which of the following statement is NOT true about SQL derived table syntax?
    A. **Temporary tables** are permitted in a derived table expression except when it is part of a create view statement.
    B. **A local variable** is permitted in a derived table expression except when it is part of a create view statement.
    C. **A correlation_name**, which must follow the derived table expression to specify the name of the SQL derived table, may omit a derived column list, whereas a view cannot have unnamed columns
    D. You can assign a value to a variable within a derived table expression.
Answer: D

85. The degree of nesting of SQL derived table is limited to?
    A. 30
    B. 64
    C. 25
    D. 255
Answer: C

3.8 List advantages of normalization

86. What are not the advantages of normalization? [Choose 2]
    A. More rows per page
    B. More rows per I/O
    C. Less rows fit in cache
    D. Searching, sorting, and creating indexes is faster, since tables are narrower, and more rows fit on a data page.
    E. You usually have more indexes per table, so data modification commands are slow.
Answer: C, E

87. Which statement describes the technique of table folding?
    A. Converting normalized data to a matrix format
    B. Converting non-normalized data to a normalized table

C. Merging a subtype/supertype relationship into one table
D. Rejoining tables from Fifth Normal Form

Answer: B

88. What are the advantages of having a normalized data model? (Choose 2)
    A. reduced redundancy
    B. minimized need for nulls
    C. reduced business rules
    E. speed up DSS system

Answer: A, B

3.9 Understand First, Second and Third Normal Form

89. Which technique would NOT cause a Third Normal Form table to become denormalized?
    A. inter-row derived column
    B. intra-row derived column
    C. duplicate column
    D. merging of a subtype/supertype relationship

Answer: D

90. Which of the following database design techniques VIOLATES third normal form?
    A. horizontally partitioning a table
    B. intra-row derived columns
    C. vertically partitioning a table
    D. composite keys

Answer: B

91. Which Normal Form is also called as "Projection-Join Normal Form"?
    A. 3rd NF
    B. 5th NF
    C. 2nd NF
    D. 4th NF

Answer: B

3.10 List denormalization techniques

92. The most prevalent denormalization techniques are?
    A. Adding redundant columns
    B. Adding derived columns
    C. Collapsing tables
    D. Duplicating tables
    E. Splitting tables
    F. All of the above

Answer: F

93. Whatever denormalization techniques you use, you need to ensure data integrity by using?
    A. Triggers

B. Application Logic
C. Batch reconciliation
D. All of the above

Answer: D

Section 4 - ANSI SQL – DDL (5 questions – 8 %)

4.1 Describe how to create tables, views, indexes, etc.

94. Which of the following is NOT true about table object?
    A. Different users can create tables of the same name.
    B. You can not create a table in another database from your current database
    C. Column names must be unique within a table
    D. There can be as many as 2,000,000,000 tables per database.

Answer: B

95. Which of the following command can create a table in another database from your current database? (Assuming newdb is another database)
    A. create table newdb..employee (emp_id int)
    B. create table newdb.employee (emp_id int)
    C. create table employee (emp_id int) in newdb
    D. create table [newdb].employee (emp_id int)

Answer: A

96. Which of the following database object you can create in a database other than the current database?
    A. Views
    B. Tables
    C. stored procedures
    D. Triggers
    E. Rules and defaults
    F. Indexes

Answer: B, F

97. You cannot create indexes on columns if datatype is
    A. bit
    B. text
    C. image
    D. All of the above
    E. None of the above

Answer: D

98. If you create a index specifying more than a column, its called a.
    A. Unique Index
    B. Key Index
    C. Composite Index
    D. Multiple Index

Answer: C

99. Given following syntax of CREATE TABE
    CREATE TABLE employee(id int, f_name char(30), l_name char(30), dob datetime)
   Which of the following create index on (id and dob column) commands are correct [Choose 2]?
    A. create index emp_idx on employee(id, dob)

B. create index emp_idx on employee(dob, idx)
C. create index emp_idx on employee("dob", "idx")
D. create index emp_idx on employee(dob and idx)

Answer: A, B (The columns in a composite index do not have to be in the same order as the columns in the create table statement)

100. View definition can NOT include which of the following?(Choose 2)
    A. where clause
    B. order by clause
    C. join
    D. distinct
    E. select into
    F. union

Answer: B, F

101. Which conditions must be true to create a nonclustered index in parallel?(choose 3)
    A. the server must be configured for parallel access
    B. the table must be partitioned
    C. the database option select into/bulkcopy/pllsort must set to true
    D. the data must reside on a user-defined segment
    E. the number of pages in the table must be at least eight times the configured of sort buffers

Answer: A, C, E.

4.2 Define column properties such as null and identity

102. NULL value means?
    A. 0
    B. Blank
    C. value unknown
    D. " "

Answer: C

103. If you omit null or not null in the create table statement, Adaptive Server always uses?
    A. NULL
    B. NOT NULL
    C. null mode defined for the database
    D. None of the above

Answer: C

104. You can define an IDENTITY column when you
    A. Create a table with a with CREATE TABLE command
    B. Create a table with a select into statement
    C. Alter table statement.
    D. All of the above

Answer: D

105. Which of the following statements are NOT true about IDENTITY column? [Choose 3]
    A. IDENTITY columns datatype can any integer type
    B. IDENTITY columns can not be datatype of numeric
    C. By default, Adaptive Server begins numbering rows with the value 0

D. By default, Adaptive Server begins numbering rows with the value 1
E. You can create an IDENTITY column from a user-defined datatype that allows null values.

Answer: B, C, E

106. You can create "hidden" IDENTITY columns automatically by?
    A. sp_dboption *database_name*, "auto identity", "true"
    B. sp_dboption *database_name*, " identity", "true"
    C. sp_dboption *database_name*, " identity column", "true"
    C. sp_dboption *database_name*, " identity column ", 1
Answer: A

4.3 Define temporary tables

107. Temporary tables are created in?
    A. tempdb database
    B. master database
    C. model database
    D. user database
Answer: A

108. SELECT * into #accounts FROM accounts
    Table created by above statement will be dropped. [Choose 2]
    A. if current session ends
    B. if user run Drop table #accounts
    C. if user run Drop table accounts
    D. None of the above
Answer: A, B

109. You can use a user-defined datatype when creating a temporary table only if the datatype exists in?
    A. userdatabase..systypes
    B. master..systyes
    C. tempdb..systypes
    D. model..systypes
Answer: C

110. To add an object permanently in tempdb, execute sp_addtype in?
    A. model database
    B. master database
    C. tempdb database
    D. user database
Answer: A

112. Which of the following statements are NOT true?
    A. System procedures such as sp_help work on temporary tables only if you invoke them from tempdb.

B. You can use user-defined datatypes in temporary tables, even if datatypes do not exist in tempdb database.
C. You can not associate rules, defaults, and indexes with temporary tables.
D. Indexes created on a temporary table disappear when the temporary table disappears.
E. You do not have to set the select into/bulkcopy option on to select into a temporary table.

Answer: B, C

113. Which of the following is FALSE regarding shareable temporary tables?
   A. dropped automatically when server is rebooted
   B. can be dropped by any user
   C. requires explicit create table permission in tempdb
   D. can be created using select into command

Answer: C

4.4 Describe ASE data types

114. Assume you want to enforce a business rule at the datatype level on a 'salesdetail' table. What step would you take during table creation to restrict the quantity column value to less than 32768?
   A. quantity bigint not null
   B. quantity smallint not null
   C. quantity tinyint not null
   D. quantity unsigned smallint not null

Answer: B

4.5 Describe different partitioning strategies

115. A _____ is a portion of a device that is defined within ASE. It is used for the storage of specific types of data such as system data, log data, and the data itself.
   A. segment
   B. table
   C. log
   D. disk

Answer: A

116. To view information about partitions use?
   A. sp_partitions
   B. sp_helpartition
   C. sp_helppartition
   D. sp_displaypartition

Answer: B

117. What is NOT the advantage of partitions?
   A. Improved scalability.
   B. Improved performance

C. Faster response time.
D. Partition not transparency to applications and users.
E. Range partitioning to manage historical data

Answer: D

118. A data partition is an independent database object with a?
    A. unique partition ID
    B. unique disk ID
    C. unique part ID
    D. None of the above

Answer: A

119. Which of the following are TRUE about data partition? [Choose 2]
    A. It is a subset of a table
    B. shares the column definitions and referential and integrity constraints of the base table.
    C. Does not share the column definitions and referential and integrity constraints of the base table
    E. It's not a subset of a table

Answer: A, B

120. Which of the following are NOT TRUE about index partition? [Choose 2]
    A. It is an independent database object identified with a unique combination of index ID and partition ID
    B. It is a subset of an index
    C. It is not a subset of an index
    D. it resides on a segment or other storage device
    E. It is an independent database object identified with a unique combination of index ID and table ID

Answer: C, E

121. Which of the partition type particularly useful for high-performance applications in both OLTP and decision-support environments like tables with constant updates, inserts, and deletes that contain a column or columns with sequential data in them?
    A. Range partitioning
    B. Hash partitioning
    C. List partitioning
    D. Round-robin partitioning

Answer: A

122. Which of the following statements are NOT True about Range partitions? [Choose 2]
    A. Range partitions are ordered
    B. Each succeeding partition must have a lower bound than the previous partition.
    C. Range partitions are not ordered
    D. Each succeeding partition must have a higher bound than the previous partition.

Answer: B, C

123. Hash partitioning is a good choice for?
    A. Large tables with many partitions—particularly in decision-support environments.
    B. Efficient equality searches on hash key columns.
    C. Data with no particular order, for example, alphanumeric product code keys
    D. All of the above

124. You can specify maximum _____ values in each list partition?
    A. 1
    B. Depends on database size
    C. 250
    D. 255
Answer: C

125. In which partition strategy Adaptive Server does not use partitioning criteria?
    A. Range partitioning
    B. Hash partitioning
    C. List partitioning
    D. Round-robin partitioning
Answer: D

126. Which of the following statements are TRUE about Round-robin partitioning? [Choose 2]
    A. Round-robin-partitioned tables have **no partition key**.
    B. Round-robin-partitioned tables have **1 partition key**.
    C. Rows are distributed randomly across all partitions.
    D. Rows are distributed semantically across all partitions.
Answer: A, C

127. Which of the following partition type can have up to 31 keys? [Choose 2]
    A. Range partitioning
    B. Hash partitioning
    C. List partitioning
    D. Round-robin partitioning
Answer: A, B

128. Which of the following partition type can have only 1 key?
    A. Range partitioning
    B. Hash partitioning
    C. List partitioning
    D. Round-robin partitioning
Answer: C

129. In which of the following statements, rows are distributed semantically across all partitions.? [Choose 2]
    A. Range partitioning
    B. Hash partitioning
    C. List partitioning
    D. Round-robin partitioning
Answer: A, C

130. Which of the following MUST be converted explicitly? (Choose 3)
    A. int and char
    B. real and varchar
    C. money and char
    D. real and int

E. datetime and real
Answer: A, B, C

131. Which of the following global variables are used to contain optimizer and partitioning information? (Choose 2)
    A. @@optgoal
    B. @@idle
    C. @@resource_granularity
    D. @@lock_timeout
Anwer: A, B
@@optgoal -- Returns the current optimization goal setting for query optimization
@@resource_granularity -- Returns the maximum resource usage hint setting for query optimization

4.6 Understand partitioning options with alter table

132. Which of the following statements are NOT TRUE? [Choose 2]
    A. You can add partitions to a hash or round-robin partitioned table.
    B. You can add partitions to list or range partitioned tables.
    C. You must drop all indexes before changing the partitioning key.
    D. You can not change partition type and partition key in a single alter command as well.
    E. You can create an unpartitioned round-robin table from a partitioned roundrobin table using alter table with the unpartition clause.
Answer: A, D

133. Which of the partition type support below commad?
    alter table discounts partition 3
    A. Range partitioning
    B. Hash partitioning
    C. List partitioning
    D. Round-robin partitioning
Answer: D

134. What is default the number of spinlocks used to protect against concurrent access of open partitions?
    A. 100
    B. 0
    C. 10
    D. 500
Answer: C

135. What is the value of default number of open partitions that Adaptive Server can access at one time?
    A. 100
    B. 0
    C. 10
    D. 500
Answer: D

136. Which of the following tasks you can action on a partition?
    A. Update statistics
    B. Update table statistics

C. Update all statistics
D. Update index statistics
E. Delete statistics
F. All of the above

Answer: F

Section 5 - ANSI SQL - DML (5 questions – 8 %)
5.1 Describe the data manipulation commands: select, insert, update, and delete, and the use of cursors

137. Which of the following are NOT DML commands [Choose 2]?
   A. SELECT
   B. TRUNCATE
   C. DELETE
   D. UPDATE
   E. INSERT
   F. DROP

Answer: B, F

138. What change is required to the following functional Transact-SQL statement to ensure that it meets the ANSI SQL-92 standard? INSERT publishers (pub_id, pub_name, city, state) VALUES ("9901", "Absolute Truth Publishing", "Chicago", "IL")
   A. Change the words INSERT and VALUES to lowercase
   B. Add the word INTO following the word INSERT
   C. Change all double quote marks to single quote marks
   D. Remove the list of columns prior to the word VALUES

Answer: B

139. Which of the following statements record affected rows in the transaction log? (Choose 2)
   A. DROP TABLE
   B. SELECT INTO.
   C. INSERT INTO.
   D. UPDATE TABLE
   E. TRUNCATE TABLE

Answer: C, D

140. Which of the following statements is FALSE for the select statement?
   A. aggregates are permitted in the where clause
   B. aggregates are permitted in the having clause
   C. subqueries are permitted in the select clause
   D. subqueries are permitted in the having clause

Answer: A

141. Which of the following statements are correct?

   A. select Publisher = pub_name, pub_id from publishers
   B. select pub_name Publisher, pub_id from publishers
   C. select pub_name as Publisher, pub_id from publishers
   D. None of the above

Answer: D

142. To reset @@textsize to the Adaptive Server default value, use?
    A. set textsize 0
    B. set textsize, 0
    C. set texsize default
    D. set textsize, "default"
Answer: A

143. Which of the following statement is NOT correct?
    A. The select statement can also include one or more expressions
    B. You can also use "*" more than once in a query
    C. local variables can be declared in a select statement
    D. The select command retrieves data stored in the rows and columns of database tables using a procedure called a query.
Answer: C

144. After executing the following commands, what will the value of @sum be?
Declare @number int, @copy int, @sum int
Select @number=10, @copy=@number, @sum=@number+200
    A. 10
    B. 100
    C. NULL
    D. 110
Answer: C

145. Given the following SQL statement, what value is returned?
declare @a int, @b int, @c int, @d int
select @a = 0, @b = null, @c = -1, @d = null
select coalesce(nullif(@a,0),@b,nullif(@c,@d),isnull(@d,@c))
    A. Null
    B. 0
    C. 1
    D. -1
Answer: D

146. Which of the following select clauses can NOT be resolved using an in-memory sort?
    A. Distinct
    B. Group by
    C. Having
    D. Union
Answer: C

147. Which of the following components of a 'select' statement will ALWAYS require a sort?
    A. Distinct
    B. Having
    C. Order by
    D. Union
    E. Union all
Answer: D

148. Which of the statement will give an error (T-SQL), if you have table definition is as below:
        CREATE TABLE employee (emp_id int,

emp_name char(50))
- A. INSERT INTO employee VALUES (1, "Abhi")
- B. INSERT INTO employee (emp_id, emp_name) VALUES (1, "Abhi")
- C. INSERT employee (emp_id, emp_name) VALUES (1, "Abhi")
- D. INSERT employee VALUES (1, "Abhi")
- E. None of the above

Answer: E

149. Which functions can avoid the divide by 0 (zero) problem in the following query? (Choose 2)
select @var_zero=0
select fname, price/@var_zero as new_amount
from table_1
- A. ceiling
- B. coalesce
- C. convert
- D. nullif

Answer: B, D

150. Which of the following operations are minimally logged? (Choose 2)
- A. checkpoint
- B. create table #temp (a char(1) not null)
- C. bcp table_name out file_name
- D. select * into new_table_name from table_name
- E. truncate table

Answer: D, E

151. Which set command is required for explicitly inserting data into an IDENTITY column?
- A. set identity_insert <table_name> on
- B. set identityinsert <table_name> on
- C. set identity_insert on <table_name>
- D. set identity_insert "table_name"

Answer: A

152. Which of the following statement is NOT true about update command?
- A. Can change single row in a table
- B. Can change group of rows in a table
- C. Can all rows in a table
- D. Can change data in more than one table at a time

Answer: D

153. What type of update would a self-join invoke?
- A. In-place
- B. Cheap
- C. Expensive
- D. Deferred

Answer: D

154. Which of the following statement are not correct [Choose 2]?
- A. If an update statement violates an integrity constraint, the update does not take place and an error message is generated

B. if an update statement modifies the same row twice, the second update is based on the new values from the first update
C. The update command is not logged.
D. You are limited to approximately 125K per update statement.

Answer: B, C

155. Which of the following statement is correct to update column, where IDENTITY column datavalue = 1
    A. update emp_transaction set emp_dept = "IT" where syb_identity = 1
    B. update emp_transaction set emp_dept = "IT" where identity = 1
    C. update emp_transaction set emp_dept = "IT" where identity_value = 1
    D. update emp_transaction set emp_dept = "IT" where identity_column = 1

Answer: A

156. Which statement is NOT TRUE regarding cursors declared in for update mode?
    A. Can retrieve data and update or delete rows through the cursor
    B. Uses update locks
    C. Disabled when the declaration of the cursor uses an aggregate function
    D. If the cursor is on a datarows locked table, the table must have a unique index

Answer: D

157. Which of the following statements are correct about cursors [Choose 2]?
    A. accesses the results of a SQL select statement one or more rows at a time
    B. Cursors allow you to modify rows or group of rows
    C. Cursors do not allow you to delete rows or group of rows
    D. Cursors do not allow you to modify rows or group of rows

Answer. A, B

158. Which of the following are correct about insensitive cursors? (Choose 2)
    A. The data set can become stale.
    B. Locks cannot be released even after the completion of the work table.
    C. Changes to the base tables are not seen by the cursor.
    D. Waiting may be required to find the next row.

Answer: A, C

159. Which statement are TRUE regarding cursors declared in for update mode [Choose 2]?
    A. Can retrieve data and update or delete rows through the cursor
    B. Uses shared locks
    C. Disabled when the declaration of the cursor uses an aggregate function
    D. If the cursor is on a datarows locked table, the table must have a unique index

Answer: A, C (FYI: Cursors uses update locks in update mode)

160. Which of the following command forces the cursor to become insensitive, even if you have declared it as semi-sensitive?
    A. update
    B. sort
    C. group by
    D. delete

Answer: B

161. Adaptive Server creates the cursor structure, when you
    A. Declare the cursor

B. Open the cursor
C. Fetch the cursor
D. Close the cursor

Answer: A

162. Cursor name can not be more than
    A. 50 characters
    B. 30 characters
    C. 20 characters
    D. None of the above

Answer: B

163. select statement in a cursor can not contain [choose 2]
    A. into clause
    B. from clause
    C. compute
    D. where clause

Answer: A, C

164. You cannot specify the for update clause if a cursor's *select_statement* contains
    A. distinct
    B. group by clause
    C. Aggregate function
    D. **union**
    E. Subquery
    F. **at isolation read uncommitted** clause
    G. All of the above

Answer: G

165. Error messages related to declaring the cursor appear during the cursor
    A. declare phase
    B. open phase
    C. fetch phase
    D. close phase

Answer: B

166. Which of the following statement are correct?
    A. You can open a cursor that is already open
    B. You can open a cursor has not been defined with the **declare cursor** statement
    C. You can reopen a closed cursor
    D. You cannot open a cursor that is already open

Answer: C, D

167. By default, fetch retrieves
    A. 0 rows at a time
    B. 1 rows at a time
    C. 100 rows at a time
    D. 2 rows at a time

Answer: B

Certification: C_SASEDP_15

168. Which of the following are true about the cursor after fetch last is executed?
    - The cursor must be closed after the last row is obtained.
    - All cursor rows are present in the cursor's worktable after the fetch last statement.
    - To resume processing the scrollable cursor, fetch first must be issued to reposition the cursor's pointer back to the first row before fetching additional rows from the cursor.
    - Two of the above
    - None of the above

Answer: B

169. Which of the following statements are true about cursor after closing cursor [Choose 3]?
    A. Does not releases the server resources held for the cursor structure
    B. keeps the query plan for the cursor
    C. Closing the cursor change its definition
    D. Closing the cursor does not change its definition
    E. Removes any remaining temporary tables

Answer. B, D, E

170. Adaptive Server removes the query plan from memory and eliminates all trace of the cursor structure, when you
    A. Close the cursor
    B. Fetch the cursor
    C. Open the cursor
    D. Deallocate the cursor

Answer: D

171. Which of the following statements are true about cursor scan [Choose 2]?
    A. If a worktable is not required, Adaptive Server performs a fetch by positioning the cursor in the base table, using the table's index keys.
    B. All scrollable cursors and insensitive non-scrollable cursors require base table to hold the cursor result set.
    C. Adaptive Server requires that cursor scans use a unique index of a table, particularly for **isolation level 0 reads**.
    D. When a worktable is used, the rows (value) retrieved with a cursor fetch statement always will be same as the values in the actual base table rows.

Answer: A, C

172. Which of the following update statement (in a cursor) is correct to update the row at the current cursor position (cursor name is pubs_crsr and table name is employee).
    A. update employee set last_name = "Vyas", where current of pubs_crsr
    B. update employee set last_name = "Vyas", where pubs_crsr current
    C. update employee set last_name = "Vyas", where pubs_crsr
    C. update employee set last_name = "Vyas", where current positions at pubs_crsr

Answer: A

173. Assume you are retrieving book titles from an ASE database into an XML document. You want the title_id and price to be translated into XML elements. Which of the following SQL statements are TRUE for the above requirement? (Choose 3)
    A. select title_id, price from titles FOR XML OPTION 'incremental=yes root=no'
    B. select title_id, price from titles FOR XML ALL

C. select title_id, price from titles FOR XML OPTION 'incremental=yes root=yes'
D. select title_id, price from titles FOR XML
E. select title_id, price from titles FOR XML SCHEMA

Answer: A, C, D

5.2 Identify important clauses of DML statements, such as where, having, order by, etc.

174. WHERE clause does not sets search condition in a
    A. SELECT
    B. UPDATE
    C. TRUNCATE
    D. DELETE
    E. INSERT

Answer: C

175. You can not specify an aggregate function in a
    A. Select clause
    B. Having clause
    C. Where clause
    D. Compute clause

Answer: C

176. Which of the following is equivalent to the clause 'where zip NOT BETWEEN 16500 and 16600'?
    A. where zip > 16600 and zip < 16500
    B. where zip >= 16599 and <= 16501
    C. where zip >= 16600 and zip <= 16500
    D. where zip < 16600 AND zip > 16500

Answer: C

177. Given the following SQL statement, what is the result?
    select title as Title, isnull(price, 0.0) as Price from titles
        where price < 7.50
    A. all rows with price < 7.50, titles with NULL for the price display a price of 0.0
    B. all rows with price < 7.50, titles with NULL for the price do not display
    C. all rows with price < 7.50, titles with NULL for the price display no value
    D. all rows with price < 7.50, titles with NULL for the price display a price of NULL

Answer: B

178. In which of the following clauses of a SELECT are subqueries permitted? (Choose 3)
    A. SELECT
    B. WHERE
    C. GROUP BY
    D. FROM
    E. ORDER BY

Answer: A, B, D

179. Which of the following are possible algorithms for doing GROUP BY [Choose 2]?
    A. Grouphasing
    B. Groupselect
    C. GroupSorted

D. Groupmatch

Answer: A, C

180. Which of the following sets conditions for group by clause?
    A. WHERE
    B. SUBQUERY
    C. HAVING
    D. LIKE

Answer: C

181. Which of the following are NOT correct group by [Choose 2]?
    A. Null values in the group by column are put into a single group
    B. You can name text, unitext, or image columns in group by
    C. The group by clause can not include columns or expressions that are not in the select list
    D. You cannot use a group by clause in the select statement of an updatable cursor

Answer: B, C

182. Which of the following are correct about Order by clause?
You can sort by
    A. column heading
    B. column name
    C. expression
    D. number representing the position of the item in the select list
    E. All of the above

Answer: E

183. Which of the following are NOT correct about order by?
    A. The maximum number of columns allowed in an order by clause is 31
    B. You can use order by on text, unitext, or image datatype columns
    C. Subqueries and view definitions can include an order by clause
    D. you cannot use a subquery in an order by list

Answer: B, C

5.3 Identify the performance and tuning aspects of DML statements, such as direct and deferred updates, etc.

184. Which of the following are techniques of direct updates [Choose 3]?
    A. Cheap direct updates
    B. In-place updates
    C. Active direct updates
    D. Expensive direct updates
    E. Performance direct updates

Answer: A, B, D

185. Which of the following are NOT true [Choose 2]?
    A. When Adaptive Server performs an in-place update, subsequent rows on the page are moved
    B. An in-place update is the fastest type of update because it makes a single change to the data page
    C. If Adaptive Server cannot perform an update in place, it tries to perform a Expensive direct update
    D. In-place updates affect only indexes whose keys are changed by the update, since the page and row locations are not changed

E. If the data does not fit on the same page, Adaptive Server performs an expensive direct update

Answer: A, C

186. Which of the following is slowest type of update?
- A. Deferred update
- B. Direct update
- C. In-place update
- D. None of the above

Answer: A

187. Which of the following is most likely to perform a direct in-place update?
- A. An update that causes a varchar column to expand
- B. An update that causes a varchar column to shrink
- C. An update to a char column that doesn't allow null values
- D. An update that changes a null value to a non-null value

Answer: C

188. What type of update would a self-join invoke?
- A. In-place
- B. Cheap
- C. Expensive
- D. Deferred

Answer: D

189. Which of the following is the most inefficient update that the query optimizer can produce?
- A. Deferred
- B. In-place
- C. Cheap
- D. Expensive

Answer: A

190. Adaptive Server performs Which update, when the update affects the index used to access the table or when the update affects columns in a unique index?
- A. Cheap
- B. Expensive
- C. In-place
- D. Deferred index

Answer: D

191. Triggers that join user tables with the deleted or inserted tables are run in?
- A. Direct mode
- B. Deferred mode
- C. Deferred Index mode
- D. None of the above

Answer: B

192. The update that uses a subquery is always performed as ?
- A. direct update
- B. deferred_varcol update
- C. deffered_index update

D. All of the above
Answer: D

193. Which two are requirements for cheap direct updates on a allpages lock table? (Choose 2)
    A. the column being updated cannot be the key, or part of the key, of a non-clustered index
    B. the column being updated cannot be the key, or a part of the key, of a clustered index
    C. the length of the data in the row cannot change
    D. one or more indexes must be unique or must allow duplicates
Answer: C, D

194. Which of the following system tools help identify deferred updates? (Choose 2)
    A. set statistics io on
    B. sp_sysmon
    C. set showplan on
    D. sp_monitor
Answer: B, C

195. Deferred updates... (Choose 2)
    A. are the slowest type of update.
    B. are implemented as deletes followed by inserts.
    C. cause row forwarding in APL tables.
    D. put fewer rows in the transaction log than cheap updates.
    E. put more rows in the transaction log than expensive updates.
Answer: A, B

196. Which of the following will cause a deferred update? (Choose 2)
    A. Update statement that uses self joins
    B. Update to a table in a join that is not the outer table
    C. Update to a primary key column with no index
    D. Update to a variable length column
Answer: A, B

197. Which of the following actions will improve query performance of an update statement by promoting direct updates to tables? (Choose 3)
    A. Prevent the use of non-key columns in the where clause when updating key columns
    B. Avoid using declarative referential integrity constraints on columns updated frequently
    C. Declare columns as NOT NULL when null values are not used in column data
    D. Reduce the use of unique indexes on tables that are frequently updated.
    E. Avoid declaring columns as fixed-length when creating tables
    F. Avoid using variable-length columns on frequently updated columns
Answer: B, C, F

5.4 Identify techniques to promote the most efficient update method

198. Which of the following messages about update are provided by showplan? [Choose 2]
    A. deferred_varcol
    B. direct_varcol
    C. direct_index_varcol
    D. deferred_index

         E. direct_index
Answer: A, D

199. Which of the following is NOT a good way to promote direct updates?
        A. Create at least one unique index on the table
        B. Use nonkey columns in the where clause of an update
        C. Declare column as "not null" for columns with no NULL values
        D. Declare small variable-length (varchar) column if it is frequently updated
Answer: D

5.5 Understand computed columns:

200. What must an expression used in a function based index contain?
        A. Base column
        B. Aggregate function
        C. Computed column
        D. Subquery
Answer: A

201. Which of the following is TRUE about materialized computed columns?
        A. Require a function based index
        B. Can be based on columns in multiple tables
        C. Physically store the computed value in the table
        D. Generate the computed value when the column is queried
Answer: C

202. Which of the following statements is TRUE about a table that is created with a column using a non-deterministic function with the 'materialized' option?
        A. Any value inserted into the computed column continues to be non-deterministic.
        B. The computed column cannot be used to create a clustered index.
        C. All values inserted into the computed column become deterministic.
        D. The function cannot be used with the materialized option when creating a table.
Answer: C

203. Which of the following characteristics are of a computed column?
        A. Materialization
        B. deterministic
        C. All of the above
Answer: C

204. Which of the following are correct about Materialized columns [Choose 2]?
        A. **Preevaluated** and stored in the table when base columns are inserted or updated
        B. The values associated with the computed columns are stored in both the data row and the index row
        C. Value evaluated each time the column is accessed
        D. None of the above
Answer: A, B

205. getdate() function is an example of?
        A. nondeterministic function

B. deterministic function
C. Both of the above
D. None of the above
Answer: A

206. Which of the following statements are true about computed columns?
- Can create defaults on computed columns
- Can not be null
- Both A and B
- Neither A nor B

Answer: D (Computed columns are nullable by default)

207. Given the following table definition:
create table sales
(stor_id char(4) not null,
order_num varchar(20) not null,
sales_date date default getdate(),
due_date as dateadd(dd, 60, sales_date) materialized)
The due_date column will have a new value each time the
    A. sales_date column is selected.
    B. due_date column is selected.
    C. sales_date column is updated.
    D. order_num column is updated.
Answer: C

208. Which of the following is NOT true about computed column [Choose 2]?
    A. You can use a virtual computed column in any constraints
    B. You cannot change a regular column into a computed column, or a computed column into a regular column
    C. You can define triggers only on non **materialized** computed columns
    D. You cannot drop or modify the base column referenced by a computed column
    E. When you change a not-null, materialized computed column into a virtual column, you must specify null in the modify clause.
Answer: A, C

209. Which of the following statements about computed columns is NOT true?
    A. Expressions can be used as column definitions.
    B. Computed columns allow results of expressions to be indexed.
    C. Computed columns can reference functions.
    D. Computed columns can reference other columns in the same table.
    E. Computed columns can be used on java columns.
Answer: E

210. Which of the following statements is NOT TRUE regarding computed columns?
    A. Regular columns can be converted into computed columns.
    B. Computed columns are either deterministic or non-deterministic.
    C. If a computed column that is part of an index is modified, the index is rebuilt.
    D. Computed columns permit the use of expressions as column definitions.
Answer: A

Section 6 - Query Access Methods (5 questions – 8 %)

6.1 Define range queries, point queries, and covered queries

211. Point queries are queries which are having?
    A. between one values to another values
    B. absolute value
    C. Non matching values
    D. None of the above
Answer: B

212. When a query is "covered" on a DOL table, the optimizer may choose a scan of the... (Choose 2)
    A. data pages without using an index.
    B. data pages using the clustered index.
    C. data pages using a nonclustered index.
    D. leaf level pages of the clustered index.
    E. leaf level pages of a nonclustered index.
Answer: D, E

213. A covered query can NOT occur on...
    A. an APL nonclustered index.
    B. an APL clustered index.
    C. a DOL clustered index.
    D. a DOL nonclustered index.
Answer: B

214. Which of the following would be best used in a heavy DSS workload environment?
    A. Primarily DOL tables with few indexes
    B. Primarily DOL tables with numerous indexes
    C. Primarily APL tables with few indexes
    D. Primarily APL tables with numerous indexes
Answer: D

215. Considering the SQL statement:: create index au_name_idx on authors (au_lname, au_fname) For which of the following queries will the optimizer NOT consider the au_name_idx index?
    A. select * from authors where au_lname="Smith"
    B. select * from authors where au_fname="Joe"
    C. select * from authors where upper(au_lname) = "SMITH"
    D. select * from authors where au_lname like "Sm%"
    E. select * from authors where au_fname like "J%"
Answer: C

216. Given the following query: select * from titles where price < 15 or title like "Assigned%" The following indexes exist on the titles table: idx1 – clustered on price idx2 – unique nonclustered on title_id idx3 – nonclustered on title idx4 – nonclustered on pub_date What indexes will the optimizer use to implement the "or" strategy? (Choose 2)
    A. idx1
    B. idx2
    C. idx3

Certification: C_SASEDP_15 44

        D. idx4

Answer: A, C

217. Which factor does the optimizer NOT consider to determine the parallel access methods to use on APL tables prior to query plan costing?
        A. partition skew
        B. configured number of worker processes
        C. existence of a clustered index
        D. table partitioning
        E. number of CPUs available

Answer: E

6.2 Explain how ASE accesses data in selects, inserts, deletes, and updates

218. If you create a table on Adaptive Server, but do not create a clustered index, the table is stored as a
        A. temp table
        B. system table
        C. heap
        D. index table

Answer: C

219. Select operation on Allpages-locked heap tables uses
        A. First column in sysindexes for the table, reads the first page into cache, and follows the next page pointers until it finds the last page of the table.
        B. The **table's OAM to locate the rows in the table**
        C. The allocation pages to locate all the rows in the table
        D. The last column in sysindexes for the table, reads the last page into cache, and follows the next page pointers until it finds the last page of the table.

Answer: A

220. Select operation on Data-only locked heap tables uses [Choose 2]
        A. First column in sysindexes for the table, reads the first page into cache, and follows the next page pointers until it finds the last page of the table.
        B. The **table's OAM to locate the rows in the table**
        C. The allocation pages to locate all the rows in the table
        D. The last column in sysindexes for the table, reads the last page into cache, and follows the next page pointers until it finds the last page of the table.

Answer: B, C

221. *On Allpages-locked heap table,* When you insert data into an allpages-locked heap table, the data row is always try to added
        A. to last page of the table
        B. to first page of the table
        C. to second page of the table
        D. to 100th page of the table

Answer: A

222. Which are the following statements are true about Conflicts during heap inserts? [Choose 2]
        A. page must be locked when the row is added
        B. lock is held until the transaction completes

C. If many users are trying to insert into an allpages-locked heap table at the same time, each insert does not wait for the preceding transaction
D. page doesn't locked when the row is added

Answer: A, B

223. How can we avoid last page conflict last-page on heaps? [Choose 3]
   A. Switching to All pages locking
   B. Creating a clustered index that directs the inserts to different pages
   C. Partitioning the table
   D. Keeping transactions long
   E. Avoiding network activity and user interaction whenever possible,once a transaction acquires locks

Answer: B, C, E

224. Which of the following statements are NOT True about Data-only-locked heap table?
   A. Adaptive Server allocates a small number of empty pages and directs new inserts to those pages using these newly allocated pages as hints.
   B. For datarows-locked tables, blocking occurs only while the actual changes to the data page are being written.
   C. Adaptive Server does not track page numbers where the inserts have recently occurred.
   D. If the page is full, Adaptive Server allocates a new page and replaces the old hint with the new page number.

Answer: C

225. When a row in a data-only-locked table is updated so that it no longer fits on the page, a process called?
   A. row forwarding
   B. table forwarding
   C. records forwarding
   D. data-row forwarding

Answer: A

226. Forwarded rows can be cleared from a table using the ?
   A. Delete table command
   B. Reorg command
   C. optdial command
   D. None of the above

Answer: B

6.3 Define I/O for a select using a non-clustered index

227. Select * from employee where lname ='Green'
   Which of the following I/O requires by above query?
   A. One read for the root level page
   B. One read for the intermediate level page
   C. One read for the leaf-level page
   D. One read for the data page
   E. All of the above

Answer: E

6.4 Define performance benefits of using indexes

228. Which of the following is a NOT performance benefit of using indexes?
    A. Avoid table scans when accessing data
    B. Target specific data pages that contain specific values in a point query
    C. Establish upper and lower bounds for reading data in a range query
    D. Avoid data page access completely, when an index covers a query
    E. Use ordered data to avoid sorts or to favor nestedloop over merge joins joins

Answer: E

229. When the transfer is complete, bcp informs you of the?
    A. Number of rows of data successfully copied
    B. Number of rows (if any) that it could not copy
    C. Total time the copy took
    D. Average amount of time, in milliseconds, that it took to copy one row
    E. Number of rows copied per second.
    F. All of the above

Answer: F

230. Which of the following statements are true about Slow bcp? [Choose 2]
    A. logs each row insert that it makes
    B. logs only page allocations
    C. used for tables that have one or more indexes or triggers
    D. copying data into tables without indexes or triggers at the fastest speed possible

Answer: A, C

231. Which of the following statements are true about Fast bcp? [Choose 2]
    A. logs each row insert that it makes
    B. logs only page allocations
    C. used for tables that have one or more indexes or triggers
    D. copying data into tables without indexes or triggers at the fastest speed possible

Answer: B, D

232. Parallel bcp process acquires the following locks?
    A. An exclusive intent lock on the table
    B. An exclusive page lock on each data page or data row
    C. An exclusive lock on index pages, if any indexes exist
    D. All of the above

Answer: D

6.5 Define logging & minimally-logged operations

233. Which of the statements are True about **select into** operations? [Choose 2]
    A. They are minimally logged
    B. They are most logged
    C. Only the allocation of data pages is tracked
    D. Every transaction is logged.

Answer: A, C

234. Which of the following commands is not a minimally logged operation?
    A. REORG REBUILD

B. TRUNCATE TABLE
C. SELECT INTO
D. DELETE

Answer: D

235. Which of the following commands are NOT True? [Choose 2]
A. The DELETE statement holds a lock on each individual row it is deleting
B. The TRUNCATE TABLE statement locks only the table and each data page.
C. The DELETE statement locks only the table and each data page.
D. The TRUNCATE TABLE statement holds a lock on each individual row it is deleting

Answer: A, B

Section 7 - Query Optimization (9 questions – 15 %)

7.1 Define the 'Or Strategy' and showplan, plus options

236. An OR strategy uses a set of index scans to limit the scan with each of the OR terms, then passes the resulting RIDs through a?
A. DistinctUnion operator
B. UnionDistinct operator
C. RidJoin operator
D. Union operator

Anser: B

237. The __ operator is a binary operator that joins two data streams, based on row IDs generated for the same source table
A. DistinctUnion operator
B. UnionDistinct operator
C. RidJoin operator
D. Union operator

Answer: C

238. If there is a possibility that one or more of the or clauses could match values in the same row, the query is resolved using the?
A. Dynamic index
B. Clustered index
C. Dynamic join
D. Union

Answer: A

239. Dynamic index (OR strategy): The total cost of the query includes?
A. The sum of the index accesses, that is, for each or clause, the cost of using the index to access the row IDs on the leaf pages of the index (or on the data pages, for a clustered index on an allpages-locked table)
B. The cost of reading the worktable and performing the sort
C. The cost of using the row IDs to access the data pages
D. All of the above

Answer: D

240. Which of the following statements are NOT True about worktable used in Dynamic index (OR strategy)?
    A. The worktable does not contain the actual data rows from the table, but rather it contains the row IDs for the matching rows.
    B. The worktable contains the actual data rows from the table and rows IDs for the matching rows.
    C. The row IDs are simply a combination of the **page number** and **row number** on that page for each of the rows.
    D. None of the above
Answer: B

241. Which of the following message displays by showplan, when the special OR strategy is used?
    A. Using *N* Matching Index Scans
    B. Using 1 Matching Index Scans
    C. Using *N* Matching OR Scans
    D. Using *N* Matching OR strategy Scans
Answer: A

242. Which of the following where clause would be considered for *OR Strategy* (multiple matching index scans)?
    A. where value between 1 and 5
    B. where value = 1
    C. where value <> 1
    D. None of the above
Answer: B

243. A query with or clauses or an in (values_list) uses a table scan if either of these conditions is true?
    A. The cost of all the index accesses is greater than the cost of a table scan
    B. At least one of the columns is not indexed
    C. The cost of all the index accesses is less than the cost of a table scan
    D. Both A and B
Answer: D

244. Which of the following technique is the default technique used to join tables and/or return rows from a table?
    A. Merge iteration
    B. Nested iteration
    C. Loop iteration
    D. None of the above
Answer: B

245. What are the valid options for the web service type in the Create Service command? (Choose 2)
    A. HTML
    B. SOAP
    C. WSDL
    D. XML
Answer: B, D

246. Showplan reports the... (Choose 3)
    A. number of logical I/Os.
    B. number of physical I/Os.
    C. table join method.

D. indexes that were considered.
E. number of worker processes.
F. data I/O size.

Answer: C, D, F

247. Showplan can tell the user the following information (Choose 2)
   A. join order
   B. if a table scan was used
   C. spid number of the user
   D. which engine was used
   E. if named cache was used

Answer: A, B

248. Which of the following is NOT provided in the output of a showplan?
   A. table name
   B. index name
   C. index keys
   D. I/O size
   E. CPU time

Answer: E

7.2 Identify optimization 'set' command tools

249. Which of the following set command reports information about physical and logical I/O and the number of times a table was accessed?
   A. set statistics io
   B. set statistics time
   C. set statistics subquerycache
   D. set statistics simulate

Answer: A

250. Which of the following set command displays the steps performed for each query in a batch?
   A. set showplan on
   B. set statistics time on
   C. set statistics io on
   D. set subquerycache on

Answer: A

251. Which of the following displays by set statistics subquerycache on command?
   A. cache hits
   B. cache misses
   C. number of rows in the cache in each subquery
   D. All of the above

Answer: D

252. set statistics time displays the time it takes to? [Choose 2]
   A. Parse
   B. Compile
   C. Normalized

D. None of the above
Answer: A, B

253. Which command forces the query to use the tables in the order specified in the from clause?
    A. set forceporder
    B. set forceplan
    C. set forcetableorder
    D. set tablecount
Answer: B

254. Which of the following statement is true about **set table count**?
    A. Increases the number of index that the optimizer considers at one time while determining join order.
    B. Increases the number of tables that the optimizer considers at one time while determining join order.
    C. Increases the number of joins that the optimizer considers at one time while determining join order.
    D. Increases the number of tables that the optimizer considers at one time while determining table order.
Answer: B

255. Which of the following statements are true? [Choose 3]
    A. By default, a query uses large I/O whenever a large I/O pool is configured.
    B. Query processor determines that large I/O would reduce the query cost.
    C. **set prefetch** toggles prefetch for query tuning experimentation.
    D. **set prefetch** fetch data from cursor.
Answer: A, B, C

256. Which of the following statement is true about sp_cachestrategy ?
    A. sets status bits to enable or disable prefetch and fetch-and-discard cache strategies.
    B. sets status bits to enable or disable procedure cache strategies
    C. sets status bits to enable or disable query cache strategies
    D. None of the above
Answer: A

257. What is the option designed to replace the 302 trace flag?
    A. set statistics plancost
    B. set option show_search_engine
    C. set option show_lio_costing
    D. option show_missing_stats
Answer: C

258. Which of the following options are stored in systabstats(Choose 3)?
    A. density values
    B. page count
    C. cluster ratios
    D. histogram values
    E. number of empty pages
    F. selectivity values
Answer: B, C, E

259. What is the default optimization timeout limit for an ad-hoc query?
A. 10
B. 0
C. 40
D. 100
Answer: A

260. The SQL statement 'set statistics plancost on'... (Choose 3)
   A. presents query plans as trees.
   B. shows estimated and actual costs per node.
   C. adjusts statistics in systabstats for the session.
   D. generates an XML document.
   E. displays plans in graphical ASCII format.
Answer: A, B, E

7.3 Use of Abstract Plans

261. Adaptive Server can generate an abstract plan for a query, and save the text and its associated abstract plan in?
   A. syscomments system table
   B. sysqueryplans system table
   C. In a user table
   D. sysstatistics system table
Answer: B

262. Adaptive server compares to saved query text to incoming SQL queries by using?
   A. Hash scan method
   B. rapid hashing method
   C. getSorted mentiod
   D. Histrograms
Answer: B

263. Which of the commands you can use to manage all abstract plans in a group? [Choose 3]
   A. sp_copy_all_qplans,
   B. sp_cmp_all_qplans
   C. sp_exportall_qplans
   D. sp_drop_all_qplans
   E. sp_helpall_qplans
Answer: A, B, D

264. Which of the command can be used to export groups of plans?
   A. sp_export_queryplangroup
   B. sp_export_qpgroup
   C. sp_export_plans
   D. sp_export_querylans
Answer: B

265. When you first install Adaptive Server, there are two abstract plan groups? [Choose 2]
   A. ap_stdout

B. ap_stdout_group
C. ap_stdin_group
D. ap_stdin

Answer: A, D

266. Which abstract plan group used by default for capturing plans?
A. ap_stdout
B. ap_stdout_group
C. ap_stdin_group
D. ap_stdin

Answer: A

267. Which abstract plan group used by default for plan association?
A. ap_stdout
B. ap_stdout_group
C. ap_stdin_group
D. ap_stdin

Answer: D

268. The full association key of an abstract plan consists of?
A. The user ID of the current user
B. The group ID of the current association group
C. The full query text
D. All of the above

Answer: D

269. Which of the following command save the the plans to the default group?
A. set plan load on
B. set plan dump on
C. set dump plan on
D. set load plan on

Answer: B

270. Which of the following command start the association mode using the default group?
A. set plan load on
B. set plan dump on
C. set dump plan on
D. set load plan on

Answer: A

271. Which of the statement is true about abstract plan?
A. Only one abstract plan group can be active for plan association at one time.
B. More than one abstract plan group can be active for plan association at one time
C. Two abstract plans group can be active for plan association at one time.
D. None of the above.

Answer: A

272. When you are capturing plans, and a query has the same query text as an already-saved plan, the existing plan is not replaced unless?
A. replace mode is enabled

B. overwrite mode is enabled
C. you have access to overwrite
D. None of the above

Answer: A

272. set plan exists check option mode can be used during query plan association to speed performance when users require?
A. Abstract plans for more than 20 queries from an abstract plan group.
B. Abstract plans for fewer than 20 queries from an abstract plan group.
C. Abstract plans for fewer than 100 queries from an abstract plan group.
D. Abstract plans for more than 100 queries from an abstract plan group.

Answer: B

273. Which of the following statement is true?
A. If set forceplan on is in effect, and query association is also enabled for the session, query association is ignored if a full abstract plan is used to optimize the query.
B. If set forceplan on is in effect, and query association is also enabled for the session, forceplan is ignored if a full abstract plan is used to optimize the query.
C. If set forceplan on is in effect, and query association is also enabled for the session, forceplan is ignored if a partial abstract plan is used to optimize the query
D. None of the above

Answer: B

274. Which of the following command will be used to enables dumping to the default abstract plans capture group server wide?
A. sp_configure "abstract plan dump", 1
B. sp_configure "abstract plan load", 1
C. set plan dump on
D. set plan load on

Answer: A

275. Which of the following command will be used to enables caching of abstract plan hash IDs server wide, when abstract plan load is enabled.
A. sp_configure "abstract plan cache", true
B. sp_configure "abstract plan cache", 1
C. sp_configure "abstract cache", 1
D. None of the above

Answer: B

276. Which of the following statements are true about abstract plan and settings? [Choose 2]
A. Enabling any of the server-wide abstract plan modes is dynamic.
B. You cannot override the serverwide modes at the session level.
C. Enabling any of the server-wide abstract plan modes is not dynamic.
D. By default configuration parameters are set to 1

Answer: A, B

277. Which of the following options is NOT available when testing a multi-table join query for the fastest possible query plan?
A. enabling and disabling join transitive closure - A
B. adding or removing statistics of non-indexed join columns

C. enabling and disabling forceplan to affect the join order
D. forcing different join methods to change the type of joins used
Answer. A

278. How many abstract plans will be generated for the following statments? -- check
User1: select type from titles where price < 50
User1: select type from titles where price < 50
User2: select type from titles where price < 50
User2: select type from titles where price < 50
    A. 1
    B. 2
    C. 3
    D. 4
Answer: C

279. Which of the following does NOT capture abstract query plans?
    A. sp_configure "abstract plan dump", 1
    B. set plan dump on
    C. dbisql
    D. isql --
Answer: D

280. Abstract Query Plans can be used for the following purposes:
    A. to identify queries that use plans, such as table scans or reformatting.
    B. to see which engines were used for the query.
    C. to see which named cache was used for the query.
    D. to identify how many physical and logical I/O took place for the query.
Answer: A

281. A "full abstract plan" includes what information? (Choose 3)
    A. I/O size
    B. parallel degree
    C. cache strategy
    D. log size
    E. dump statistics
Answer: A, B, C

7.4 Determine if the optimizer selected serial or parallel access

282. Which of the following statements are true about Parallel query execution? [Choose 2]
    A. The total amount of work performed by the query running in parallel is greater than the amount of work performed by the query running in serial
    B. The total amount of work performed by the query running in parallel is less than the amount of work performed by the query running in serial
    C. The response time by the query running in parallel is shorter than the response time by the query running in serial
    D. The response time by the query running in parallel is not shorter than the response time by the query running in serial
Answer: A, C

283. Which of the following is not a parallel method?
    A. Hash-based table scan
    B. Hash-based nonclustered index scan
    C. Partition-based scan, either full table scans or scans positioned with a clustered index
    D. Merge table scan
    E. Range-based scan during merge joins
Answer: D

284. Hash-based table scans are used only for?
    A. Inner query in a join
    B. Subquery in a join
    C. Union
    D. Outer query in a join
Answer: D

285. Which of the following statements benefits from parallelism? (Choose 2)
    A. Select
    B. Insert
    C. Update
    D. Delete
    E. Create index
Answer: A, E

286. In Hash-based index scans; each worker process navigates higher levels of the index and read the?
    A. Disk pages
    B. Leaf-level pages of the index
    C. Intermediate-level pages of the index
    D. None of the above
Answer: B

287. A parallel query's degree of parallelism is the?
    A. Number of family processes used to execute the query
    B. Number of worker processes used to execute the query
    C. Number of tables used to execute the query
    D. Number of disks used to execute the query
Answer: B

288. The number of worker processes depends on?
    A. The values to which of the parallel configuration parameters or the session-level limits
    B. The number of partitions on a table (for partition-based scans)
    C. The level of parallelism suggested by the optimizer
    D. The number of worker processes that are available at the time the query executes
    E. None of the above
    F. All of the above
Answer: F

289. Which of the following statements are true about max parallel degree? [Choose 2]
    A. It must be equal to or less than number of worker processes
    B. It must be equal to or grater than number of worker processes

C. It must be equal to or greater than max scan parallel degree.
D. It must be equal to or less than max scan parallel degree.

Answer: A, C

290. Which of the following statements are true about max scan parallel degree? [Choose 2]
   A. It must be equal to or less than number of worker processes
   B. It must be equal to or grater than number of worker processes
   C. It must be equal to or greater than max parallel degree.
   D. It must be equal to or less than max parallel degree.

Answer: A, D

291. Any Transact-SQL command that requires data row sorting can benefit from?
   A. Parallel sorting techniques
   B. Serial sorting techniques
   C. Hash scan techniques
   D. All of the above

Answer: A

292. Which of the following commands can benefit from parallel sorting techniques?
   A. Create index commands
   B. Queries that use the order by clause
   C. Queries that use distinct
   D. Queries that perform merge joins requiring sorts
   E. Queries that use union (except union all)
   F. Queries that use the reformatting strategy
   G. All of the above

Answer: G

293. In Parallel sorting strategy for a merge join with statistics on a join column
   A. Histogram statistics are used for the distribution map
   B. sysqueryplan statistics are used for the distribution map
   C. The input table is sampled to build the map
   D. None of the above

Answer: A

294. Which of the following is NOT TRUE for the query optimizer?
   A. Examines queries and statistics about the tables, indexes and column names in the query
   B. Predicts the cost of using alternative methods to access the required data
   C. Selects the query plan that is the least costly in terms of time
   D. Reduced contention on temp tables --

Answer: D

295. Which of the following conditions must be TRUE for parallel processing to be considered by the optimizer? (Choose 2)
   A. The max parallel degree parameter must be 2 or greater.
   B. The max parallel degree parameter must be 1 or greater.
   C. The number of worker processes parameter must be 2 or greater.
   D. The number of worker processes parameter must be 1 or greater.

Answer: A, C

296. Which of the following are TRUE about parallel processing? (Choose 2)

A. requires multiple engines
B. allows the task to use more ASE resources
C. ASE supports vertical & horizontal parallelism
D. optimizer cannot estimate response time for parallel plans

Answer: B, C

7.5 Define Procedure Cache & explain how stored procedures are processed

297. As users execute stored procedures, Adaptive Server looks in ___ for a query plan to use?

A. Procedure cache
B. Query cache
C. Buffers
D. None of the above

Answer: A

298. If no plan is in memory procedure cache, or if all copies are in use, the query tree for the procedure is read from the?

A. sysprocedures table
B. sysplans table
C. sysprocedurecahce table
D. None of the above

Answer: A

299. Which of the following is default procedure cache size?

A. 255 bytes
B. 3271 memory pages
C. 1000 memory pages
D. 1 memory page

Answer: B

300. The percentage of times the server finds an available plan in cache is called?

A. cache hit percentage
B. cache ratio
C. find ratio
D. cache hit ratio

Answer: D

Q. Which of the statement is true?

A. Keeping a high cache hit ratio for procedures in cache improves performance.
B. Keeping a less cache hit ratio for procedures in cache improves performance.
C. Keeping a high cache hit ratio for procedures in cache decrease performance.
D. None of the above

Answer: A

301. How to calculate Procedure cache size?

A. Procedure cache size = (Max # of concurrent users) * (Size of largest plan) * 1.25
B. Procedure cache size = (Total # of concurrent users) * (Size of Average plan) * 1

C. Procedure cache size = (Total # of concurrent users) * (Size of largest plan) * 1
D. Procedure cache size = (Max # of concurrent users) * (Size of Average plan) * 1.25
Answer: A

302. How to calculate *Minimum procedure cache size needed?*
    A. Minimum procedure cache size needed = (# of total procedures) *(Average plan size)
    B. Minimum procedure cache size needed = (# of main procedures) *(Average plan size)
    C. Minimum procedure cache size needed = (Max # of concurrent users) * (Size of largest plan) * 1.25
    D. Minimum procedure cache size needed = (# of main procedures) *(largest plan size)
Answer: B

303. Given that 3 users are simultaneously executing the same procedure, what is the minimum number of compiled copies of the procedure that can be found in the procedure cache?
    A. 1
    B. 2
    C. 3
    D. 0
Answer: 3

7.6 Identify factors for setting Prefetch at the Query-Level

304. **Prefetch** Specifies the?
    A. I/O size to use for the scan of a stored table.
    B. I/O size to use for the merge of a stored table.
    C. I/O size to use for the scan of a database.
    D. None of the above.
Answer: A

305. How many Abstract Query Plan groups exist at installation?
    A. 1
    B. 2
    C. 4
    D. 8
    E. 16
Answer: 2

7.7 Identify Query Degradation

306. Which of the following configuration parameter can be turned on during boot-time and run-time to allocate all the shared memory up to 'max memory' with the least number of shared memory segments?
    A. 'allocate min shared memory'
    B. 'allocate max shared memory'
    C. 'allocate max memory'
    D. 'allocate min memory'
Answer: B

7.8 Identify tasks for which internal working tables are created in tempdb or in memory

307. Which of the statements are true about WORKTABLES? [Choose 3]
    A. Worktables are automatically created in tempdb by Adaptive Server for merge joins, sorts, and other internal server processes.
    B. Worktables are shared
    C. Disappear as soon as the command completes
    D. Worktables are never shared
    E. Worktables are automatically created in master datbase by Adaptive Server for merge joins, sorts, and other internal server processes.
Answer: A, C, D

7.9 Design queries to take maximum advantage of optimizer features

308. What are the advantages of new optimization techniques and query execution operators?
    A. On-the-fly grouping and ordering operator support using in-memory sorting and hashing for queries with group by and order by clauses
    B. Hash and MergeJoin operator support for efficient join operations
    C. index union and index intersection strategies for queries with predicates on different indexes
    D. All of the above
Answer: D

7.10 Describe how the optimizer analyzes search arguments (SARG)

309. What do you call a predicate in a query's WHERE clause that can be used to locate a row via an index?
    A. RowID
    B. SARG
    C. Function
    D. Parameter
ANswer: B

310. Which of the following is not a valid SARG?
    A. where name like 'sch%'
    B. where name like 's%h'
    C. where name like '%aaf'
    D. where name like 'joh?'
Answer: C

7.11 Identify factors of Subquery Optimization

311. Which of the following optimizations can be used to improve performance?
    A. Flattening
    B. Materializing
    C. Short circuiting
    D. Caching subquery results
    E. All of the above

Certification: C_SASEDP_15

Answer: E

312. A subquery introduced with in, any, or exists cannot be flattened if? [Choose 4]
    A. The subquery is correlated and contains one or more aggregates.
    B. The subquery is in the select list or in the set clause of an update statement.
    C. The subquery is the not the outermost subquery in a case expression.
    D. The subquery is connected to the outer query with or
    E. The subquery is not a part of an isnull predicate
    F. If the subquery computes a scalar aggregate, materialization rather than flattening is used.
Answer: A, B, D, F

313. Which of the following are **Flattening methods**?
    A. A regular join
    B. Semi-join
    C. A unique reformat
    D. A duplicate elimination sort optimization
    E. All of the above
Answer: E

Section 8 - Stored Procedures and Triggers (4 questions – 6 %)

8.1 Write and tune stored procedures and triggers

314. Which of the following statement is correct to execute a stored procedure *employee_proc*?
    A. employee_proc
    B. execute employee_proc
    C. exec employee_proc
    D. All of the above
Answer: D

315. Which of the following statements is NOT TRUE about Create procedure *with recompile* (optional)?
    A. A plan always accessed by procedure cache
    B. A new plan is created each time the procedure is executed.
    C. Using execute procedure *with recompile* many times can adversely affect the procedure cache performance
    D. If you use select * in your create procedure statement, the procedure, even if you use the with recompile option to execute, does not pick up any new columns added to the table. You must drop the procedure and re-create it.
Answer: A

316. Which of the following statements are NOT TRUE about stored procedure? [Choose 2]
    A. stored procedure can take parameters
    B. Can not call other procedures
    C. Return a status value to a calling procedure or batch to indicate success or failure and the reason for failure
    D. Return values of parameters to a calling procedure or batch
    E. Can not be executed on remote Adaptive Servers
Answer: B, E

317. How to protect source text of a stored procedure? [Choose 2]

A. By restricting select permission on the text column of the syscomments table to the creator of the procedure and the System Administrator.
B. Hide the source text using sp_helprotect (system procedure).
C. Hide the source text using sp_hidetext (system procedure).
D. By restricting select permission on the id column of the syscomments table to the creator of the procedure and the System Administrator.

Answer: A, C

318. The maximum number of arguments for stored procedures is?
    A. 2048
    B. 255
    C. 30
    D. 1
Answer: A

319. Which of the following statement are TRUE about stored procedures? [Choose 3]
    A. You can assign default parameters in Create Procedure statement.
    B. Adaptive Server ignores the extra parameters passed in stored procedure.
    C. You can not use wildcard characters in the stored procedure parameter
    D. you can declare null as the default value for individual parameters of stored procedure.
    E. You can drop individual group of a procedure
Answer: A, B, D

320. Which of the following statements are NOT TRUE about stored procedure? [Choose 3]
    A. Maximum levels of nesting is 30.
    B. Maximum levels of nesting is 16.
    C. The current nesting level is stored in the @@level global variable.
    D. The current nesting level is stored in the @@nestlevel global variable.
    E. You can call another procedure by name.
    F. You can not call another procedure by a variable name in place of the actual procedure name.
Answer: A, C, F

321. Which of the following statements is NOT True about stored procedures?
    A. You can use some of the set command options inside a stored procedure.
    B. You can not use some of the set command options inside a stored procedure.
    C. The set option remains in effect during the execution of the procedure and most options revert to the former setting at the close of the procedure.
    D. Only the dateformat, datefirst, language, and role options do not revert to their former settings.
Answer: B

322. proc role function checks whether the procedure was executed by a user with a
    A. sa_role
    B. so_role
    C. ss_oper privileges
    D. All of the above
Answer: D

323. If more than one error occurs during execution of a stored procedure

A. The status with the highest absolute value is returned.
B. The status with the lowest absolute value is returned.
C. value 0 is returned
D. value 1 is returned

Answer: A

324. Which of the following features or commands is NOT allowed in a stored procedure?
   A. create temporary table
   B. use of dynamic SQL
   C. create rule
   D. remote server access through CIS

Answer: C

325. Which of the following statements are NOT TRUE about stored procedures?
   A. You can combine create procedure statements with other statements in the same batch.
   B. You can not create view, default, rule, trigger, procedure in side create procedure command.
   C. You can create view, default, rule, trigger, procedure in side create procedure command.
   D. Within a stored procedure, you cannot create an object, drop it, and then create a new object with the same name.
   E. The maximum number of parameters in a stored procedure is 255.

Answer: A, C

326. Which of the following system procedure is used to get a report of the objects referenced by a procedure?
   A. sp_helpreference
   B. sp_depends
   C. sp_helpprocedure
   D. None of the above

Answer: B

327. Which of the following statements is TRUE?
   A. Query trees are created at EXEC PROC time, and stored in the database.
   B. Query trees are created at CREATE PROC time, and kept only in memory.
   C. Query plans are created at CREATE PROC time, and kept only in memory.
   D. Query trees are created at CREATE PROC time, and stored in the database.
   E. Query plans are created at CREATE PROC time, and stored in the database.

Answer: D

328. When a stored procedure is created as create procedure... with recompile, which statements are TRUE? (Choose 2)
   A. default optimization behavior of stored procedure is changed
   B. query plan is NOT re-usable after the execution of procedure
   D. previously stored query plan in sysprocedures is used for execution
   E. user need to recompile the stored procedure prior to execution

Answer: A, B

8.2 Define query plans and the procedure cache

Please check in Section **7.5 Define Procedure Cache & explain how stored procedures are processed**

8.3 Define triggers and their usage

329. Which of the following statements are true about triggers? [Choose 2]
   Trigger "fires" only
   A. Before the data modification statement has completed.
   B. After the data modification statement has completed.
   C. After Adaptive Server has checked for any datatype, rule, or integrity constraint violation
   E. Before Adaptive Server has checked for any datatype, rule, or integrity constraint violation
Answer: B, C

330. Which of the statements is true if Adaptive Server detects a sever error?
   A. Entire transaction is rolled back.
   B. Entire transaction is committed.
   C. Partial transaction is rolled back.
   D. Partial transaction is committed.
Answer: A

331. Which type of triggers you can not be create in ASE?
   A. Insert Trigger
   B. Delete Trigger
   C. Update Trigger
   D. All of the above
Answer: D

332. When do triggers fire?
   A. Before the log records are written
   B. Only if the key column(s) are affected
   C. Once for each row affected by the data modification
   D. Once regardless of the number of rows affected
Answer: D

333. Which of the following command is correct to disable all the triggers on a table?
   A. ALTER TABLE <table_name> DISABLE ALL TRIGGER
   B. ALTER TABLE <table_name> DISABLE TRIGGER
   C. ALTER TABLE <table_name> DISABLE TRIGGERS
   D. None of the above
Answer: B

334. Which of the following commands can be executed in trigger?
   A. rollback trigger [with raiserror_statement]
   B. rollback trigger [with raiserror_statement]
   C. Both A and B
   D. None of the above
Answer: C

335. Which of the following statement is NOT TRUE about *if update* clause in triggers?
   A. *if update* clause tests for an insert or update to a specified column (not for delete).
   B. For updates, *if update* clause evaluates to true when the column name is included in the set clause of an update statement, even if the update does not change the value of the column.

C. For updates, *if update* clause evaluates to false when the column name is included in the set clause of an update statement and if the update does not change the value of the column.
D. You can specify more than one column, and you can use more than one if update clause in a create trigger

Answer: C

336. if update(*column_name*) clause is not true for?
   A. Default assigns a value to a column
   B. Explicit NULL
   C. Implicit NULL
   D. All of the above

Answer: C

337. Which of the following statements is NOT TRUE?
   A. By default, a trigger call itself recursively (**self-recursion**)
   B. A **rollback transaction** in a trigger at any nesting level rolls back the effects of each trigger and cancels the entire transaction
   C. A **rollback trigger** affects only the nested triggers and the data modification statement that caused the initial trigger to fire
   E. @@nestlevel global variable stores the current nesting level.

Answer: A

338. Which of the following commands trun on self-recursion for triggers?
   A. EXEC sp_dboption '<name of db>', 'recursive triggers', 1
   B. EXEC sp_dboption '<name of db>', 'recursive triggers', true
   C. EXEC sp_dboption '<name of db>', 'triggers 'recursive ', true
   D. EXEC sp_dboption '<name of db>', ' self recursion ', true

Answer: B

339. Which of the following statements are NOT TRUE about triggers?
   A. You cannot create a trigger on a view or on a temporary table, though triggers can reference views or temporary tables.
   B. You cannot use triggers that select from a text column or an image column of the inserted or deleted table
   C. The writetext command, cause a trigger to fire.
   D. The truncate command, cause a trigger to fire.

Answer: C, D

340. Which of the following statements are TRUE in reference to the use of Adaptive Server procedure cache? (Choose 3)
   A. The configuration parameter 'procedure cache size' represents a percentage of memory used by Adaptive Server.
   B. Procedure cache is used for sort operations.
   C. An amount of procedure cache memory is needed for each scrollable cursor.
   D. Query plans for triggers and dynamic sql are stored in the procedure cache.
   E. Changing the size of procedure cache requires a re-boot of Adaptive Server.

Answer: B, C, E

Section 9 - Transact-SQL Statements (5 questions – 8 %)

9.1 Use of Sybase-specific Transact-SQL commands, such as functions, programming commands such as if and while, local and global variables

341. Which of the following can be including in CASE expression?
    A. WHEN
    B. CASE
    C. THEN
    D. coalesce
    E. nullif
    F. All of the above

Answer: F

342. coalesce examines a series of values (*value1*, *value2*, ..., *valuen*) and returns the?
    A. first null value
    B. first non-null value
    C. last non-null value
    D. All of the above

Answer: B

343. Which of the following statements are NOT TRUE about nullif expression? [Choose 2]
    A. compares two values
    B. if the values are equal, nullif returns a null value
    C. if the values are equal, nullif returns value 1
    D. If the two values are not equal, nullif returns the value of the first value.
    E. If the two values are not equal, nullif returns value 0

Answer: C, E

344. A series of statements enclosed by begin and end is called?
    A. Execute block
    B. Statement block
    C. Begin block
    D. End block

Answer: B

345. Which of the following keyword control the operation of the statements inside a while loop? [Choose 2]
    A. break
    B. end
    C. continue
    D. start

Answer: A, C

346. If two or more while loops are nested, break exits?
    A. to the next outermost loop
    B. to the first outermost loop
    C. to the last outermost loop
    D. None of the above

Answer: A

347. Which of the following keyword causes unconditional branching to a?

A. system loop
B. user-defined label
C. user-defined cursor
D. All of the above

Answer: B

348. Which of the following statements are NOT true? [Choose 2]
    A. The *error_number* is placed in the global variable *@@error*, which stores the error number most recently generated by Adaptive Server.
    B. Error numbers for user-defined error messages must be less than 17,000
    C. If the *error_number* is between 17,000 and 19,999, and *format_string* is missing or empty (" "), Adaptive Server retrieves error message text from the sysmessages table in the master database.
    D. Local variables used for raiserror messages can be integer
    E. The severity level of all user-defined error messages is 16, which indicates that the user has made a nonfatal mistake.
    F. The length of the *format_string* alone is limited to 255 bytes; the maximum output length of *format_string* plus all arguments is 512 bytes.

Answer: B, D

349. Which of the following statements are true about local variables? [Choose 2]
    A. A subquery that assigns a value to the local variable *must* return only one value.
    B. A subquery that assigns a value to the local variable *can* return more than one value and it will assign all the values to local variables.
    C. When you declare a variable, it has the value NULL
    D. When you declare a variable, it has the value 0

Answer: A, C

350. Which of the following statements is NOT true about the case expression?
    A. It is a T-SQL extension.
    B. It can be used anywhere an expression can be used.
    C. At least one clause must return a non-null value.
    D. It can execute statements.
    E. It must return values of a compatible datatype.

Answer: D

351. The "print" command can be supplied with argument list. Placeholders indicate where arguments are inserted and must be in the format of %n!, where n is an integer between_____.
    1-10
    1-20
    1-60
    1-100

Answer: B

9.2 Describe 'scrollable cursors'
Please read following sections:
1.2 Identify aspects of insensitive/semi-sensitive scrollable cursors
5.1 Describe the data manipulation commands: select, insert, update, and delete, and the use of cursors

9.3 Identify guidelines for SARGs

352. If you think a particular query plan is unusual, you can use ___ to determine why the optimizer made the decision.
    A. errorlog file
    B. dbcc traceon(302)
    C. dbcc traceon(100)
    D. sysqueryplan
Answer: B

353. Which of the following statement is not true about SARGs?
    A. getdate() is converted to literal values before optimizations and can not be optimized.
    B. system functions object_id and object_name are not converted to literal values before optimizations and can not be optimized.
    C. between Converted to >= and <= clauses
    D. int_column = convert(int, "77") will be processed as int_column = 77
Answer: A

354. Join transitive closure is not performed for?
    A. Non-equijoins
    B. Equijoins that include an expression
    C. Equijoins under an *or* clause
    D. **Outer joins**
    E. Joins across subquery boundaries
    F. Joins used to check referential integrity or the with check option on views
    G. Columns of incompatible datatypes
    H. All of the above
Answer: H

355. Which of the following statements are NOT TRUE about Statistics for SARGS?
    A. Histograms are used to determine the selectivity of the SARG, that is, how many rows from the table match a given value.
    B. Density values, measuring the density of keys in the index.
    C. Cluster ratios that measure the fragmentation of data storage and the effectiveness of large I/O.
    D. You can display these statistics using optdiag.
    E. Histograms can not be used to determine the selectivity of the SARG.
Answer: E

356. When you create an index, a histogram is created on the ___?
    A. Last column of the index.
    B. Last column of the table.
    C. First column of the table.
    D. First column of the Index.
Answer: D

357. Which of the statements is true about Histogram?
    A. The histogram stores information about the distribution of values in the index.
    B. The histogram stores information about the distribution of index of the table.
    C. The histogram stores information about the distribution of values in the column.
    D. All of the above
Answer: C

Certification: C_SASEDP_15   68

358. Which of the following are types of Histogram? [Choose 2]
    A. Frequency cell
    B. Range cell
    C. Index cell
    D. density cell
Answer: A, B

359. Which of the following is true for Density value?
    A. Density is a measure of the max proportion of duplicate keys of index.
    B. Density is a measure of the average proportion of duplicate keys of index.
    C. Density is a measure of the min proportion of duplicate keys of index.
    D. Density is a measure of the max proportion of duplicate columns of table.
Answer: B

360. Which of the following statements are true for Density value? [Choose 3]
    A. It varies between 1 and 100.
    B. An index with N rows whose keys are unique has a density of 1/N.
    C. An index whose keys are all duplicates of each other has a density of 0.
    D. For indexes with multiple keys, density values are computed and stored for each prefix of keys in the index.
    E. An index with N rows whose keys are unique has a density of N/1.
Answer: B, D

361. When the optimizer estimates costs for the query, the two factors it considers are ?
    A. cost of physical I/O
    B. cost of logical I/O
    C. Bothe A and B
    D. None of the above
Answer: C

362. The total cost of accessing a table can be expressed as?
    A. All physical IOs * 18 + All logical IOs * 2
    B. All physical IOs * 2 + All logical IOs * 18
    C. All physical IOs + All logical IOs
    D. All physical IOs * All logical IOs
Answer: A

363. Which of the following statement are true for Check constraint?
    A. You can declare a check constraint to limit the values users insert into a column in a table
    B. Check constraints are useful for applications that check a limited, specific range of values.
    C. A check constraint specifies a *search_condition* that any value must pass before it is inserted into the table.
    D. All of the above
Answer: D

364. Which of the following WHERE clauses could be made SARGs through the use of a function-based index? (Choose 2)
    A. where col1 = @var
    B. where upper(col1) = "SMITH"
    C. where substring(col1,2,2) = "bc"
    D. where col1 = col2

F. where col1 <> 10
Answer: B, C

365. Which statements are TRUE about 'join transitive closure' (JTC)? (Choose 2)
    A. JTC is disabled by default.
    B. JTC generates additional search arguments, which are not specified in the query but which are logically implied, for consideration by the optimizer.
    C. JTC generates additional join clauses, which are not specified in the query but which are logically implied, for consideration by the optimizer.
    D. JTC forces the optimizer to choose a more efficient join order.
    E. JTC reduces the time needed for query optimization.
    F. JTC cannot be disabled.
Answer: A, C

Note: By default, join transitive closure is not enabled at the server level, since it can increase optimization time. You can enable join transitive closure at a session level with set jtc on. The session-level command overrides the server-level setting for the enable sort-merge joins and JTC configuration parameter. By default, merge joins are not enabled at the server level. When merge joins are disabled, the server only costs nested-loop joins, and merge joins are not considered. To enable merge joins server-wide, set enable sort-merge joins and JTC to 1. This also enables join transitive closure.

10.2   Describe traditional Sybase data integrity mechanisms such as rules and defaults

366. Which of the following statements are true about Default? [Choose 3]
    A. You can create a default in the current database only.
    B. You can bind a default to a system datatype.
    C. You can bind a default to a timestamp column.
    D. You can bind a default to an IDENTITY column or to a user-defined datatype with the IDENTITY property, but Adaptive Server ignores such defaults and assigns value that is greater than the last IDENTITY value assigned.
    E. If a default already exists on a column, you must remove it before binding a new default.
Answer: A, D, E

367. Which of the following statements are NOT TRUE about RULE?
    A. The rule definition can contain any expression that is valid in a where clause, and can include arithmetic operators, comparison operators, like, in, between, and so on.
    B. The rule definition can reference any column or other database object directly.
    C. Built-in functions that do not reference database objects *can* be included.
    D. use **sp_bindrule** to link the rule to a column or user-defined datatype.
Answer: B

Section 11 - Transaction Management and Locking (5 questions – 8 %)

11.1   Describe the behavior of transactions and transaction management commands

368. Which of the following statement is true about savepoint? [Choose 2]
    A. savepoint is a marker that a user puts inside a transaction to indicate a point to which it can be rolled back.

B. savepoint is a marker that a user puts inside a transaction to indicate a point to which it can be commit.
C. savepoint can not be used in a transaction.
D. rollback transaction or save transaction does not affect Adaptive Server and does not return an error message if the transaction is not currently active.

Answer: A, D

369. You can use certain data definition language commands in transactions by running?
A. sp_dboption *database_name*,"ddl in tran", true
B. sp_dboption *database_name*,"ddl commands ", true
C. set *database_name*,"ddl commands ", true
D. set *database_name*,"ddl in transaction", true

Answer: A

370. If global variable @@transtate return 0 value, it means?
A. Transaction succeeded. The transaction completed and committed its changes.
B. Transaction in progress. A transaction is in effect; the previous statement executed successfully.
C. Statement aborted. The previous statement was aborted; no effect on the transaction.
D. Statement aborted. The previous statement was aborted; no effect on the transaction.

Answer: B

371. If global variable @@transtate return 2 value, it means?
A. Transaction succeeded. The transaction completed and committed its changes.
B. Transaction in progress. A transaction is in effect; the previous statement executed successfully.
C. Statement aborted. The previous statement was aborted; no effect on the transaction.
D. Statement aborted. The previous statement was aborted; no effect on the transaction.

Answer: C

372. Which of the following statements are NOT TRUE about global variable @@transtate?
A. Adaptive Server clears @@transtate after every statement.
B. It changes @@transtate only in response to an action taken by a transaction.
C. Syntax and compile errors **do not** affect the value of @@transtate.
D. Do not keeps track of the current state of a transaction.

Answer: A, D

373. The @@trancount global variable keeps track of the?
A. rows count
B. tansaction counts
C. Current nesting level for transactions
D. None of the above

Answer: C

374. Which of the following statements are true for @@trancount global variable?
A. initial implicit or explicit begin transaction sets @@trancount to 1.
B. Each subsequent begin transaction decrements @@trancount, and a commit transaction increments it.
C. Nested transactions are not committed unless @@trancount equals 1.
D. Nested transactions are not committed unless @@trancount equals 0.

Answer: A, C

375. Which of the following provides a list of all locked accounts?

A. sp_lock
B. sp_locklogin
C. sp_logdevice
D. sp_dropglockpromote
E. sp_familylock

Answer: B

sp_lock : Reports information about processes that currently hold locks.
sp_locklogin: Locks an Adaptive Server account so that the user cannot log in, or displays a list of all locked accounts.

376. The column blk_spid from the stored procedure sp_who indicates..
    A. process ID of the task or transaction holding the lock. --
    B. process ID of the task or transaction being blocked.
    C. process ID of the task or transaction requesting the lock.
    D. process ID of the task or transaction viewing the lock.

Answer: A

The blk_spid or block_xloid column shows the process ID of the task or transaction holding the lock or locks.

11.2 Describe behavior of locks

377. The process that is blocked by the lock sleeps until the lock is released. This is called?
    A. sleep lock
    B. lock held
    C. lock contention
    D. All of the above

Answer: C

378. Which of the following statements is true for deadlock?
    A. The transaction with the least accumulated CPU time is killed and all of its work is rolled back.
    B. The transaction with the max accumulated CPU time is killed and all of its work is committed.
    C. The transaction with the least accumulated CPU time is killed and all of its work is committed.
    D. None of the above

Answer: A

379. Adaptive server supports locking at the?
    A. Table level
    B. Page level
    C. row level
    D. All of the above

Answer: D

380. Allpages locking locks?
    A. Data pages
    B. Index pages
    C. Bothe A and B
    D. None of the above

Answer: C

381. When a query updates a value in a row in an allpages-locked table, the data page is locked with?
    A. an exclusive lock

        B. A shared lock
        C. Both A and B
        D. None of the above
Answer: A

382. Which of the following is NOT TRUE about locks?
        A. In datapages locking, entire data pages are still locked, but index pages are not locked.
        B. In datarows locking, row-level locks are acquired on individual rows on data pages. Index rows and pages are not locked.
        C. Adaptive Server uses table locks whenever possible to reduce **contention** and to **improve concurrency**.
        D. Page or row locks are less restrictive (or smaller) than table locks.
Answer: C

383. Which of the following statements are NOT TRUE for shared locks?
        A. Adaptive Server applies shared locks for update operations.
        B. If a shared lock has been applied to a data page or data row or to an index page, other transactions can not acquire a shared lock
        C. By default, Adaptive Server releases shared locks after it finishes scanning the page or row
        D. Adaptive Server applies shared locks for read operations.
        E. No transaction can acquire an exclusive lock on the page or row until all shared locks on the page or row are released.
Answer: A, B

384. Which of the following statements are NOT TRUE for update locks?
        A. Adaptive Server applies an update lock during the initial phase of an update, delete, or fetch (for cursors declared for update) operation while the page or row is being read.
        B. The update lock allows shared locks on the page or row.
        C. The update lock allows update on the page or row.
        D. The update lock allows exclusive on the page or row.
        E. Update locks help avoid deadlocks and lock contention.
Answer: C, D

385. Which of the following statements are NOT true?
        A. In general, read operations acquire shared locks, and write operations acquire exclusive locks.
        B. For operations that delete or update data, Adaptive Server applies page-level or row-level exclusive and update locks only if the column used in the search argument is part of an index.
        C. If no index exists on any of the search arguments, Adaptive Server must acquire a table-level lock.
        D. If no index exists on any of the search arguments, Adaptive Server must acquire a row-level exclusive lock.
Answer: D

386. Intent lock can be?
        A. An exclusive lock
        B. A shared lock
        C. Both A and B
        D. None of the above
Answer: C

387. A create nonclustered index command acquire?

A. shared table lock
B. An exclusive table lock
C. Intent lock
D. All of the above
Answer: A

388. A create clustered index command acquire?
    A. shared table lock
    B. An exclusive table lock
    C. Intent lock
    D. All of the above
Answer: B

389. Adaptive Server sets a ____ **lock** to indicate that a transaction is next in the queue to lock a table, page, or row.
    A. Demand
    B. Intent
    C. shared
    D. None of the above
Answer: A

390. Which of the following statements are true for latches? [Choose 2]
    A. Latches are non transactional synchronization mechanisms used to guarantee the physical consistency of a page.
    B. Latches are transactional synchronization mechanisms used to guarantee the physical consistency of a page.
    C. Latches are used for **datapages** and **datarows** locking
    D. Latches are used for allpages locking
Answer: A, C

391. Which of the following locking allows **select** and **readtext** queries to silently skip all **rows** or **pages** locked with incompatible locks?
    A. Intent
    B. Demand
    C. Readpast
    D. Shared
Answer: C

392. Given a DOL table with the following characteristics - 1000 data pages - clustered index with three levels - nonclustered index with three levels Which access method will result in the fewest logical I/Os for a point query?
    A. a full table scan
    B. using the clustered index to access the data pages
    C. using the nonclustered index to access the data pages
    D. using a covered query on the nonclustered index
Answer: B

393. At which level are intent locks placed?
    A. row
    B. page

C. table
D. extent
Answer: C

394. Which isolation level is most likely to cause deadlocks?
   A. isolation level 0
   B. isolation level 3
   C. isolation level 1
   D. isolation level 2
Answer: B

11.3   Describe transaction logging; lock blocking, diagnosis and resolution of deadlocks [PnT-Locking]

395. Every change to a database, whether it is the result of a single update statement or a grouped set of SQL statements, is recorded in the system table?
   A. sysstatistics
   B. syslogs
   C. sysprocedures
   D. syscomments
Answer: B

11.4   Describe the effect of transaction isolation levels

396. Which of the following global variable displays current transaction mode?
   A. @@tranmode
   B. @@tranchanged
   C. @@mode
   D. @@chained
Answer: B

397. Which of the following command set chained mode enable?
   A. set chained on
   B. set chained 1
   C. set tranchained on
   D. set chainedmode on
Answer: A

398. Which of the default transaction mode in ASE?
   A. Unchained mode
   B. Chained mode
   C. All of the above
   D. None of the above
Answer: A

399. Which of the following statements are true about chained mode?
   A. Although chained mode implicitly begins transactions with data retrieval or modification statements, you can nest transactions only by explicitly using begin transaction statements.
   B. Implicitly begins a transaction before any data retrieval or modification statement.

C. You must still explicitly end the transaction with commit transaction or rollback transaction.
D. All of the above
Answer: D

400. Which of the following isolation level for data-only locked tables?
    A. Level 0
    B. Level 1
    C. Level 2
    D. Level 3
Answer: C

401. Which of the following variable displays current isolation level of T-SQL session?
    A. @@isolationlevel
    B. @@isolation
    C. @@isolation_level
    D. None of the above
Answer: B

402. Which of the isolation level requires in ANSI SQL Standard?
    A. Level 0
    B. Level 1
    C. Level 2
    D. Level 3
Answer: D

403. Which of the isolation level supported by ASE?
    A. Level 0
    B. Level 1
    C. Level 2
    D. Level 3
Answer: B

404. Which of the following statements is NOT TRUE about Isolation level precedence?
    A. The holdlock, noholdlock, and shared keywords take precedence over the at isolation clause and set transaction isolation level option, except in the case of isolation level 0.
    B. The holdlock, noholdlock, and shared keywords take precedence over the at isolation clause and set transaction isolation level option, except in the case of isolation level 3.
    C. The at isolation clause takes precedence over the set transaction isolation level option
    D. The transaction isolation level 0 option of the set command takes precedence over the holdlock, noholdlock, and shared keywords.
Answer: B

405. Which of the following isolation level is not supported by cursors?
    A. Level 0
    B. Level 1
    C. Level 2
    D. Level 3
Answer: C

406. The Sybase system procedures always operate at?

A. Isolation Level 0
B. Isolation Level 1
C. Isolation Level 2
D. Isolation Level 3

Answer: B

407. User stored procedures operate at the?
A. Isolation 1
B. Isolation 2
C. Isolation level of the transaction that executes it.
D. Isolation Level 0

Answer: C

408. If a trigger fires in a transaction at level 0, Adaptive Server sets the trigger's isolation level to?
A. Isolation 1
B. Isolation 2
C. Isolation Level 0
D. Isolation Level 3

Answer: A

11.5 Define methods for reducing lock contention

409. Which of the following statements are true to reduce lock contention between update and select queries?
A. Use datarows or datapages locking for tables with lock contention due to updates and selects.
B. Select only needed columns. Avoid using *select ** when all columns are not needed by the application.
C. If tables have more than **32** columns; make the first 32 columns the columns that are most frequently used as search arguments and in other query clauses.
D. Use any available predicates for select queries.
E. All of the above.

Answer: E

11.6 Describe how ASE resolves a deadlock

410. ASE notified which message number in case of deadlock?
A. 100
B. 1207
C. -1
D. 1205

Answer: D

Section 12 - Joins, Subqueries, and Unions (4 questions – 6 %)

12.1 Define the different types of joins

411. How can you force a merge join? (Choose 2)
   A. set sort_merge on
   B. abstract query plans
   C. set forceplan on
   D. set nl_join 0

Answer: B, D

12.2   Describe the union and union all command

412. Which of the following command returns a single result set that combines the results of two or more queries?
   A. Union
   B. Outer join
   C. OR
   D. WHERE

Answer: A

413. The total number of tables that can appear on all sides of a union query is?
   A. 50
   B. Unlimited
   C. 10
   D. 256

Answer: D

414. Which of the following statements are allowed only at the end of the union statement to define the order of the final results or to compute summary values? [Choose 2]
   A. GROUP BY
   B. ORDER BY
   C. COMPUTE
   D. HAVING

Answer: B, C

415. Which of the following statements are allowed only within individual queries and cannot be used to affect the final result set?
   A. GROUP BY
   B. ORDER BY
   C. COMPUTE
   D. HAVING

Answer: A, D

416. The default evaluation order of a SQL statement containing union operators is?
   A. left-to-right
   B. right-to-right
   C. top-to-bottom
   D. bottom-to-top

Answer: A

12.3   Describe subqueries

417. You can next up to ___ subqueries in a statement?

A. 50
B. Unlimited
C. 256
D. 100

Answer: 50

418. Which of the following operator is an existence check and equivalent to in?
    A. >all
    B. >any
    C. =any
    D. All of the above

Answer: C

Section 13 - Optimizer Statistics (3 questions – 6 %)

13.1 Describe table-level and distribution statistics

419. When you create an index, a histogram is generated for the?
    A. leading column in the table.
    B. leading column in the index.
    C. unused column in the index.
    D. All of the above.

Answer: B

420. The statistics are stored in the
    A. systabstats
    B. sysstatistics
    C. Both A and B
    D. None of the above.

Answer: C

421. Which of the following statement is true for
    update statistics *table_name (column_name, column_name...)* ?
    A. Generates statistics for only these columns.
    B. Generates statistics for all columns in all indexes on the table.
    C. Generates a **histogram** for the leading column in the set, and multi column **density values** for the prefix subsets.
    D. Generates statistics for all columns of the index.

Answer: C

422. Which of the following statement is true for
    update statistics *table_name*
    A. Generates statistics for all columns of the index.
    B. Generates statistics for all columns of a table.
    C. Generates statistics for all columns in all indexes on the table.
    D. Generates statistics for the leading column in each index on the table.

Answer: D

423. Which of the following statements are true about statistics? [Choose 3]

A. Dropping an index drops the statistics for the index.
B. Dropping an index does not drop the statistics for the index.
C. If two users attempt to create an index on the same table, with the same columns, at the same time, one of the commands may fail due to an attempt to enter a duplicate key value in sysstatistics.
D. You can drop and re-create indexes without affecting the index statistics, by specifying 1 for the number of steps in the with statistics clause to create index.
E. Truncating a table delete the column-level statistics in **sysstatistics**.
F. If you want to remove the statistics after dropping an index, you must explicitly delete them with delete statistics.

Answer: B, C, F

424. Which of the following statement is true about table Systabstats? [Choose 2]
A. Stores information about the table or index as an object, that is, the size, number of rows, and so forth.
B. It is updated by query processing, data definition language, and update statistics commands.
C. Stores information about the values in a specific column.
D. It is not updated by query processing, data definition language, and update statistics commands.

Answer: A, B

425. Which of the following statement is true about table Sysstatistics? [Choose 2]
A. Stores information about the table or index as an object, that is, the size, number of rows, and so forth.
B. It is updated by It is updated by data definition language and update statistics commands.
C. Stores information about the values in a specific column.
D. It is updated by data definition language and update statistics commands.

Answer: C, D

426. Which of the following displays statistics from the systabstats and sysstatistics tables?
A. sp_who
B. sp_help
C. syscomments
D. optdiag utility

Answer: D

13.2 Define the different types of statistics, such as cluster ratios, density values, and histograms

427. Which of the following is used to compute the data page cluster ratio?
A. Data row size
B. Forwarded row count
C. Date Page CR Count:
D. All of the above

Answer: C

428. For a table, the data page cluster ratio measures the?
A. Effectiveness of large I/O for accessing the table.
B. Packing and sequencing of leaf-level index pages on index extents.

C. Packing and sequencing of pages on extents.
D. None of the above.
Answer: C

429. For an index, the data page cluster ratio measures the?
    A. Effectiveness of large I/O for accessing the table using this index.
    B. Packing and sequencing of leaf-level index pages on index extents.
    C. Packing and sequencing of pages on extents.
    D. None of the above.
Answer: A

430. For an index, the index page cluster ratio measures the?
    A. Effectiveness of large I/O for accessing the table using this index.
    B. Packing and sequencing of leaf-level index pages on index extents.
    C. Packing and sequencing of pages on extents.
    D. None of the above.
Answer: B

431. In APL tables, immediately after the clustered index is created, the data page cluster ratio is?
    A. 0
    B. < 1
    C. 1
    D. > 1
Answer: C

432. In DOL tables, If extents contain unused pages, the data page cluster ratio is?
    A. 0
    B. < 1
    C. 1
    D. > 1
Answer: B

433. Which of the following store information about the distribution of values in a column?
    A. Index page
    B. Clustered ratio
    C. Histogram
    D. None of the above

434. Which of the following statements are true about Histogram? [Choose 3]
    A. A histogram is a set of cells in which each cell has a weight. Each cell has an upper bound and a lower bound, which are distinct values from the column.
    B. The weight of the cell is a floating-point value between 0 and 1
    C. The weight of the cell is a floating-point value between 1 and 10
    D. Represents the fraction of rows in the table within the range of values, if the operator is >=,
    E. Represents the number of values that match the step, if the operator is =.
Answer: A, B, E

435. Adaptive Server uses _____, where the number of rows represented by each cell is approximately equal?
    A. equi histograms
    B. equi-height histograms

C. equi-length histograms
D. equi-cell histograms

Answer: B

13.3 Describe simulated statistics

436. Which commands can be used to specify number of histogram steps for data distribution statistics? (Choose 2)
   A. create table
   B. create index
   C. update statistics
   D. drop index
   E. set statistics i/o

Answer: B, C

Note: number of histogram steps defines the default for all create index and update index statistics commands for new histograms. The default value for number of histogram steps is 20

437. Which of the following data page cluster ratio values represent an unfragmented table?
   A. zero
   B. one
   C. two
   D. zero

Answer: B

438. Which tools or methods can be used to determine the index page cluster ratio for a particular index? (Choose 2)
   A. optdiag utility
   B. direct query against sysattributes
   C. direct query against sysstatistics
   D. derived_stat()

Answer: A, D

Certification: C_SASEDP_15

IMPORTANT: DEMP QUESTION PAPER

Question: 1
Which of the following statistics are NOT captured by QP Metrics?
A. Elapsed time
B. Logical I/O
C. Physical I/O
D. Subquery caching
Answer: D

Question: 2
In which of the following partition types is data distributed in order of operation?
A. Hash
B. Range
C. List
D. Round robin
Answer: D

Question: 3
Which of the following are TRUE about the cursor fetch statement? (Choose 2)
A. The row number starts at 0.
B. If fetch behavior is not specified, the next row is assumed by default.
C. For a scrollable cursor, @@rowcount cannot exceed the total number of rows in the result set.
D. @@fetch_status=0 implies the last fetch was successful.
Answer: B, D

Question: 4
Which function measures the amount of change in the data distribution since update statistics?
A. data_pages
B. count
C. datachange
D. used_pgs
Answer: C

Question: 5
Global indexes can be clustered on
A. Round robin partitioned tables only.
B. Round robin or range partitioned tables.
C. Round robin, range or hash partitioned tables.
D. List partitioned tables only.
Answer: A

Question: 6
The allrows_oltp optimization goal considers
A. Bushy trees.
B. Hash joins.
C. Merge joins.
D. Nested loop joins.
E. Parallelism.
F. All optimization methods.
Answer: D

Question: 7
An operator tree is displayed as a result of which command?
A. set showplan on
B. set option show_lio on
C. set statistics plancost on

D. set option show long
Answer: C

Question: 8
Metrics capture gives the administrator the ability to see which query performed (Choose 2)
A. The most physical I/O.
B. The least logical I/O.
C. A table scan.
D. A clustered index scan.
E. Large I/O.
Answer: A, B

Question: 9
Which type of join requires outer and inner tables sorted in join key order?
A. Nested Loop
B. Merge
C. Hash
D. N-ary Nested Loop
Answer: B

Question: 10
In which of the following clauses of a SELECT are subqueries permitted? (Choose 3)
A. SELECT
B. WHERE
C. GROUP BY
D. FROM
E. ORDER BY
Answer: A, B, D

Question: 11
Which operator returns a single result set that combines the result of two or more queries?
A. IN
B. UNION
C. LIKE
D. AND
Answer: B

Question: 12
Which of the following is TRUE about correlated subqueries?
A. The two statements can be resolved independently of one another.
B. The subqueries can be run in any order.
C. The subqueries can be rewritten as joins.
D. The inner query is dependent on the outer query.
Answer: D

Question: 13
Isolation level 2
A. Decreases the duration of shared locks.
B. Decreases the duration of exclusive locks.
C. Increases the duration of shared locks.
D. Only applies to All Pages locking schemes.
Answer: C

Question: 14
What lock type will prevent a series of shared locks from blocking an exclusive lock?
A. Demand
B. Intent

C. Next-key
D. Range-key
E. update
Answer: A

Question: 15
When using the READPAST keyword, when do rows/pages with conflicting locks get read?
A. As soon as blocking locks are released
B. At the end of each read operation
C. At the end of the transaction
D. Depends on the value of lock wait
E. Never
Answer: E

Question: 16
Locks escalate from (Choose 2)
A. Latch to page.
B. Latch to row.
C. Page to table.
D. Row to page.
E. Row to table.
Answer: C, E

Question: 17
Which of the following options is FALSE about unchained mode in ASE?
A. A commit tran is always implied for every transaction.
B. Unchained mode is the default mode in ASE
C. The server does not issue the begin tran implicity
D. The value of @@tranchained is 0
Answer: A

Question: 18
Given the following command sequence:
create table publishers
(pub_id char(4) not null,
pub_name varchar(40) null,
city varchar (20) null,
state char(2) null)
go
create default def_ca as CA
go
create default def_ny as NY
go
sp_bindefault def_ca, publishers.state
go
sp_bindefault def_ny, publishers.state
go
insert publishers (pub_id, pub_name, city, state)
values (0736, New Age Books, Berkeley, null)
go
What will be the result? (Choose 2)
A. The state column will have the value CA.
B. The state column will have the value NY.
C. The sp_bindefault def_ca command will generate an error.
D. The sp_bindefault def_ny command will generate an error.

E. The state column will be null.
F. The insert command will generate an error.
Answer: D, E
Question: 19
Which of the following structures can be used to enforce entity integrity? (Choose 2)
A. Trigger
B. sp_primarykey
C. Check constraint
D. References constraint
E. Primary key constraint
Answer: A, E
Question: 20
What methods are available to enforce entity integrity?
A. Check constraints
B. Primary key constraints
C. Reference constraints
D. Rules
Answer: B
Question: 21
Which normal forms require that non-key columns be functionally dependent solely on the primary key? (Choose 3)
A. First
B. Second
C. Third
D. Fourth
E. BoyceCodd
Answer: C, D, E
Question: 22
What is the effect of creating a stored procedure with recompile?
A. The stored procedure will not pass output parameters
B. The stored procedure will be re-optimized each time it is executed
C. The stored procedure query tree will not be saved in the sysprocedures table
D. The stored procedure will not fire any triggers
Answer: B
Question: 23
Which of the following statements are TRUE regarding the rollback trigger statement? (Choose 2)
A. May modify the value of @@error
B. Allows the trigger to finish executing before rolling back
C. Rolls back the entire transaction that contains the trigger
D. Rolls back work done by the trigger and the firing statement
E. Rolls back only work done by the trigger, not the firing statement
Answer: A, D
Question: 24
Which of the following commands can be used to receive a return status from a stored procedure?
A. select @status = exec proc_name @parm1
B. exec @status = proc_name @parm1
C. exec proc_name @parm1
select @status = @parm1
D. exec proc_name @parm1

select @status = @@sqlstatus
E. exec pro_name @status = @parm1
Answer: B

Question: 25
When a view is used within a procedure, how is the view referenced within the query tree?
A. By object id
B. By the view name
C. By the internal binary reference number assigned to derived objects
D. By the names of the objects referenced by the view when it was created
Answer: A

Question: 26
Which of the following statistics is NOT simulated?
A. Cache pools
B. Max parallel degree
C. Table level statistics
D. Column statistics
Answer: D

Question: 27
What is the command-line utility for viewing, writing and simulating statistics?
A. sybmigrate
B. optdiag
C. sqldbgr
D. bcp
Answer: B

Question: 28
What is used to determine how many rows qualify for the search argument?
A. Histogram
B. Forwarded rows
C. Data cluster ratio
D. Index cluster ratio
Answer: A

Question: 29
The modulos operator (%) CANNOT be used on the _____ datatype.
A. Tinyint
B. Money
C. Float
D. Smallint
Answer: B

Question: 30
Which of the following statements are FALSE about identity columns? (Choose 2)
A. The identity_insert command allows the user to put in duplicate values in the column.
B. The identity column can use any integer as its datatype.
C. When the identity column is created a unique index is also created.
D. The identity column can be updated.
Answer: C, D

Question: 31
Which of the following is NOT allowed in a view definition?
A. Aggregate function
B. Reference to another view
C. Subquery
D. Order by

Answer: D

Question: 32
What conditions must be met before altering the partition strategy of a table from round-robin to a range partitioned table?
A. Additional partitions must be added to the round-robin table
B. Table must be un-partitioned before changing partition strategy
C. Table data must be truncated
D. Table indexes must be dropped

Answer: D

Question: 33
What will happen if a table uses range partitioning, and a row is inserted with a partition key outside of the defined ranges?
A. The row will be inserted into the first partition
B. The row will be inserted into the last partition
C. The insert will fail with an error
D. A new partition is created

Answer: C

Question: 34
Which index definition would result in the following query being optimized as a covered query for an APL table? select emp_id, phone from employees where emp_id=322016
A. Create clustered index idx1 on employees(emp_id)
B. Create nonclustered index idx2 on employees(emp_id)
C. Create clustered index idx1 on employees(emp_id, phone)
D. Create nonclustered index idx2 on employees(emp_id, phone)

Answer: D

Question: 35
Which of the following are required for a covered query? (Choose 2)
A. The index must be clustered.
B. The index must be nonclustered.
C. The index must be composite.
D. All columns in the query must be found in a single index.
E. Leading column of the index must be listed in the WHERE clause.

Answer: B, D

Question: 36
Slow bcp will occur when (Choose 2)
A. Tables have one or more indexes.
B. Tables have one or more triggers.
C. Tables have one or more stored procedure.
D. Tables contain defaults.

Answer: A, B

Question: 37
Which of the following statements record affected rows in the transaction log? (Choose 2)
A. DROP TABLE
B. SELECT INTO.
C. INSERT INTO.
D. UPDATE TABLE
E. TRUNCATE TABLE

Answer: C, D

Question: 38
What must an expression used in a function based index contain?

A. Base column
B. Aggregate function
C. Computed column
D. Subquery
Answer: A

Question: 39
Assume no function-based indexes are in use. Which 'where' clauses would allow ASE to position by key using the global nonclustered index on the 'name' column? (Choose 2)
A. where left(name, 3) = "Bob"
B. where name like "%Bob"
C. where name like "Bob%"
D. where name like upper("Bob%")
E. where upper(name) like "BOB%"
Answer: C, D

Question: 40
After executing the following commands, what will the value of @sum be?
Declare @number int, @copy int, @sum int
Select @number=10, @copy=@number, @sum=@number+100
A. 10
B. 100
C. NULL
D. 110
Answer: C

Question: 41
Which of the following statements is TRUE about a table that is created with a column using a non-deterministic function with the 'materialized' option?
A. Any value inserted into the computed column continues to be non-deterministic.
B. The computed column cannot be used to create a clustered index.
C. All values inserted into the computed column become deterministic.
D. The function cannot be used with the materialized option when creating a table.
Answer: C

Question: 42
Given the following SQL statement, what value is returned?
declare @a int, @b int, @c int, @d int
select @a = 0, @b = null, @c = -1, @d = null
select coalesce(nullif(@a,0),@b,nullif(@c,@d),isnull(@d,@c))
A. Null
B. 0
C. 1
D. -1
Answer: D

Question: 43
Which of the following are legal in dynamic SQL using the EXEC command? (Choose 2)
A. BEGIN TRAN statements
B. ROLLBACK TRAN statements
C. Using a local variable to supply a table name
D. Using a local variable to supply an SQL keyword
Answer: C, D

Question: 44
Which of the following functions does the Query Optimizer perform? (Choose 3)
A. Examines queries and statistics about the tables, indexes, and column names in a query

B. Enables and controls parallel processing
C. Manages locking structures and schemes
D. Predicts cost of using alternative methods to access required data
E. Manipulates data structure utilization and arranges efficient device utilization
F. Selects the query plan that is the least costly in terms of time
Answer: A, D, F

Question: 45
Which is the correct order for executing a SQL statement in ASE 15?
A. sql statement => parse => query tree=> query plan => optimize =>execution
B. sql statement => query tree => parse =>optimize=> query plan=>execution
C. sql statement => query tree => parse => query plan => optimize =>execution
D. sql statement => parse => query tree=> optimize=> query plan=>execution
Answer: D

Question: 46
Which of the following is TRUE about materialized computed columns?
A. Require a function based index
B. Can be based on columns in multiple tables
C. Physically store the computed value in the table
D. Generate the computed value when the column is queried
Answer: C

Question: 47
Which of the following are TRUE about the UNION operator? (Choose 2)
A. Each query must select the same number of arguments.
B. Renaming column headings are not allowed in select statements.
C. The result set column headings come from the first query.
D. By default, duplicate values are included in the result set.
Answer: A, C

Question: 48
Which of the following is equivalent to the clause 'where zip NOT BETWEEN 16500 and 16600'?
A. where zip > 16600 and zip < 16500
B. where zip >= 16599 and <= 16501
C. where zip >= 16600 and zip <= 16500
D. where zip < 16600 AND zip > 16500
Answer: C

Question: 49
What type of update would a self-join invoke?
A. In-place
B. Cheap
C. Expensive
D. Deferred
Answer: D

Question: 50
Which of the following is the most inefficient update that the query optimizer can produce?
A. Deferred
B. In-place
C. Cheap
D. Expensive
Answer: A

Question: 51
In the process of optimizing a query where TableA.col1 = TableB.col2 and TableB.col2 =

TableC.col3, the optimizer will create an additional clause stating TableA.col1 = TableC.col3. This is known as
A. Hash joining.
B. SARG transitive closure.
C. Join transitive closure.
D. LOP creation.
E. Partition elimination.
Answer: C

Question: 52
Which set command shows the details of useful statistics missing from SARG/Join columns.
A. set statistics plancost
B. set option show_missing_stats
C. set option show_best_plan
D. set option show_search_engine
Answer: B

Question: 53
How can you detect if a query is missing statistics useful for optimization?
A. Query systatistics and systabstats after running the query
B. Run update statistics before running the query
C. Query monProcessActivity after running the query
D. Run set option show_missing_stats before running the query
Answer: D

Question: 54
Which of the following conditions cause showplan to include a worktable?
A. Union all
B. Reformatting
C. Nonclustered scan
D. Partition elimination
Answer: B

Question: 55
Which of the following statements are TRUE regarding parallel processing? (Choose 2)
A. A single worker process must be available for each partition
B. Hash based partition scans are no longer available
C. Horizontal and vertical parallelism are possible
D. The number of worker processes used will be reduced incrementally
Answer: C, D

Question: 56
Which of the following is NOT a reason for using Abstract Query Plan?
A. Use pre-upgrade abstract plan for degraded query on new release
B. Identify queries that use plans such as table scans or reformatting
C. Apply abstract plans to restrict queries to run on specific engines
D. Used the abstract plan to avoid long optimization times
E. Specifying full/partial plans for poor performing queries
Answer: C

Question: 57
Which of the following costing formulas is used by the Adaptive Server optimizer to help determine the estimated cost of a table scan?
A. Number of data pages in the table
B. Number of index levels
C. Number of rows per data page
D. Number of OAM pages

Answer: A

Question: 58
Which set option will show the optblocks that have timed out?
A. set option show_lop
B. set option show_elimination
C. set option show_missing_stats
D. set option show

Answer: D

Question: 59
Which of the following select clauses can NOT be resolved using an in-memory sort?
A. Distinct
B. Group by
C. Having
D. Union

Answer: C

Question: 60
Which of the following components of a 'select' statement will ALWAYS require a sort?
A. Distinct
B. Having
C. Order by
D. Union
E. Union all

Answer: D

Question: 61
What is the optimizer method of converting a subquery into a join?
A. Flattening
B. Short circuiting
C. Subquery caching
D. Materializing

Answer: A

Question: 62
Which of the following conditions must be TRUE for the optimizer to choose a full merge join? (Choose 2)
A. Indexes must be present on the join column of each table
B. Minimallylogged operations must be enabled
C. Parallelism must be enabled
D. The join condition must be equality (=)

Answer: A, D

Question: 63
Which join type consists of an alternating sequential scan of the inner and outer tables?
A. Hash
B. Merge
C. Nested Loop
D. N-ary Nested Loop

Answer: B

Question: 64
Which statement is NOT TRUE regarding cursors declared in for update mode?
A. Can retrieve data and update or delete rows through the cursor
B. Uses update locks
C. Disabled when the declaration of the cursor uses an aggregate function

D. If the cursor is on a datarows locked table, the table must have a unique index
Answer: D
Question: 65
Which of the following statements is NOT true of local variables?
A. Their name must begin with @
B. They are local to the batch or stored procedure where they are declared
C. They can be declared in a select statement
D. They cannot have a datatype of text or image
Answer: C
Question: 66
The print command can be supplied with the argument list. Arguments can be any datatype except _____.
A. money
B. varchar
C. char
D. text
Answer: D
Question: 67
Which statement describes the technique of table folding?
A. Converting normalized data to a matrix format
B. Converting non-normalized data to a normalized table
C. Merging a subtype/supertype relationship into one table
D. Rejoining tables from Fifth Normal Form
Answer: B
Question: 68
Which functions can avoid the divide by 0 (zero) problem in the following query? (Choose 2)
select @var_zero=0
select fname, price/@var_zero as new_amount
from table_1
A. ceiling
B. coalesce
C. convert
D. nullif
Answer: B, D
Question: 69
An index created by defining a unique constraint (Choose 2)
A. Cannot contain null values.
B. Enforces referential integrity.
C. Creates a clustered index by default.
D. Creates a non-clustered index by default.
E. Cannot be dropped with the 'drop index' statement.
F. Can only be applied to one column per table unless a table level constraint is specified.
Answer: D, E
Question: 70
Which one of the following constraints enforces domain integrity?
A. Primary key constraint
B. Check constraint
C. Foreign key constraint
D. Unique constraint
Answer: B
Question: 71

The bulk copy utility (bcp) (Choose 3)
A. Can do logged bulk inserts into a table.
B. Can do minimally logged bulk inserts into a table.
C. Can not insert values into an identity column.
D. Can not copy data from a view.
E. Can insert data into a particular partition.
Answer: A, B, E

Question: 72
Which of the following operations are minimally logged? (Choose 2)
A. checkpoint
B. create table #temp (a char(1) not null)
C. bcp table_name out file_name
D. select * into new_table_name from table_name
E. truncate table
Answer: D, E

Question: 73
Which of the following statements are TRUE about covered queries? (Choose 2)
A. Covered queries can only be used with nonclustered indexes on APL tables.
B. They are not valuable for clustered indexes on DOL tables.
C. The index must contain all the columns named in the select list.
D. The use of a clustered index is usually faster.
E. The index pages contain all the necessary data required for the query.
Answer: C, E

Question: 74
If the customers table has a nonclustered index on (cust_id and cust_name) then what kind of query is the following? (Choose 2)
select cust_id, cust_name
from customers
where cust_name = ABC, Inc.
A. covered
B. noncovered
C. matching index scan
D. non-matching index scan
Answer: A, D

Question: 75
When testing queries for performance, what is an advantage of using the (index table_name) clause in an SQL statement as shown in the following example?
select count(*) from titles (index titles)
A. Forces the optimizer to select any clustered index that may exist for the table
B. Forces the optimizer to select a table scan
C. Forces the optimizer to disregard table partitions when determining cost of execution
D. Forces the optimizer to select only a nonclustered indexes that may exist for the table
Answer: B

Question: 76
Which of the following statements about distribution statistics are TRUE? (Choose 2)
A. Contain exactly 20 step values
B. May be maintained for each column of each table
C. Form an equalheight histogram
D. Null values stored in the first step
E. May be modified as long as their total weights equal exactly 1

Answer: B, D

Question: 77

What optimizer statistics can be simulated? (Choose 2)
A. Cache size
B. Column distribution
C. Largest partition size
D. Data page cluster ratio

Answer: A, C

Question: 78

If no statistics are available for closed interval search (ex. Col > x and col < y), the optimizer selects which default density value?
A. 10
B. 25
C. 33
D. 50
E. 75

Answer: B

Question: 79

Which of the following commands affect a query plan?
A. set parallel_degree
B. set nocount
C. set forceplan
D. set prefetch
E. set merge_join

Answer: B

Question: 80

An N-ary join is (Choose 2)
A. A type of hash join.
B. A type of nested loop join.
C. A type of sort merge join.
D. An optimization for joins of tables with no qualifying join indexes.
E. An optimization for joins of three or more tables.

Answer: B, E

Question: 81

At what point of optimization is the best access method chosen?
A. Normalization
B. Pre-Processing
C. The Prep Phase
D. The Search Engine Phase

Answer: D

Question: 82

Which of the following statements are TRUE about the query represented by the partial abstract plan shown below? (Choose 2)

"(i_scan titles)
(prop titles
(prefetch 16))"

A. The query will table scan the table named titles.
B. The query will use the index named titles.
C. The query will use an index, but is free to choose the cheapest.
D. The query must use the MRU caching strategy.
E. The query must use the LRU caching strategy.

F. The query will use the 16KB I/O size wherever possible.
Answer: C, F

Question: 83
Large I/O for a query is useful for (Choose 2)
A. Point queries that return a single row.
B. Range queries using a clustered index.
C. Small tables (< 8 pages) with no suitable index.
D. Large tables (> 1000 pages) with no suitable index.
Answer: B, D

Question: 84
The optimizer choosing to create a clustered index on the copied rows of an inner table during a join is known as the
A. Greedy strategy.
B. HYPS strategy.
C. MRU strategy.
D. reformatting strategy.
Answer: D

Question: 85
Parallelism can improve the performance of all of the following SQL statements EXCEPT: (Choose 2)
A. A large number of rows using order by.
B. Deletes that remove a large number of rows.
C. Updates that affect a large number of rows.
D. Large number of rows using group by.
E. Merge joins.
Answer: B, C

Question: 86
Non-privileged users require set tracing permissions to execute which command?
A. set forceplan
B. set option show
C. sp_cachestrategy
D. set prefetch
Answer: B

Question: 87
Join query performance can be improved by (Choose 2)
A. Putting an index on a join column.
B. Using join clauses as per ANSI-92 syntax.
C. Joining temporary tables in a separate SQL batch.
D. Joining temporary tables in a SQL batch.
Answer: A, C

Question: 88
Using the with check option in a view definition
A. Ensures the where condition is enforced on delete.
B. Ensures the where condition is enforced on update.
C. Ensures the where condition is enforced on select.
D. Is necessary for views based on outer joins.
E. Forces the view to be read only.
Answer: B

Question: 89
Which of the following are TRUE about NULLS? (Choose 2)

A. Columns are defined to either allow NULLs or disallow NULLs.
B. For numeric values, NULL is equal to zero.
C. For character values, NULL is equal to (space character).
D. Two NULLs are not considered to be equal.
Answer: A, D

Question: 90
A table stores financial data and numerous reports are run based on fiscal quarter. Which partitioning strategy would achieve the best results with the least amount of setup?
A. A round-robin partitioned table, partitioned on the date column
B. A range partitioned table, partitioned on the date column
C. A list partitioned table, partitioned on the date column
D. A hash partitioned table, partitioned on the date column
Answer: B

Question: 91
What does the following statement do? select * into #t from myDb..myTable
A. Creates a table in tempdb
B. Creates a temporary table in myDb
C. Will be fully logged
D. Will only succeed if "select into/bulkcopy/pllsort" is set on myDb
Answer: A

Question: 92
Which partition mode does NOT support partition elimination?
A. Hash
B. List
C. Range
D. Roundrobin
Answer: D

Question: 93
Given the following SQL statement, what is the result?
select title as Title, isnull(price, 0.0) as Price
from titles
where price < 7.50
A. all rows with price < 7.50, titles with NULL for the price display a price of 0.0
B. all rows with price < 7.50, titles with NULL for the price do not display
C. all rows with price < 7.50, titles with NULL for the price display no value
D. all rows with price < 7.50, titles with NULL for the price display a price of NULL
Answer: B

Question: 94
Where can you specify an aggregate function in a query? (Choose 3)
A. Select clause
B. Group by clause
C. Where clause
D. Order by clause
E. Having clause
F. Compute clause
Answer: A, E, F

Question: 95
Given the following table definition:
create table sales
(stor_id char(4) not null,
order_num varchar(20) not null,

sales_date date default getdate(),
due_date as dateadd(dd, 60, sales_date) materialized)
The due_date column will have a new value each time the
A. sales_date column is selected.
B. due_date column is selected.
C. sales_date column is updated.
D. order_num column is updated.
Answer: C

Question: 96
What change is required to the following functional Transact-SQL statement to ensure that it meets the ANSI SQL-92 standard? INSERT publishers (pub_id, pub_name, city, state) VALUES ("9901", "Absolute Truth Publishing", "Chicago", "IL")
A. Change the words INSERT and VALUES to lowercase
B. Add the word INTO following the word INSERT
C. Change all double quote marks to single quote marks
D. Remove the list of columns prior to the word VALUES
Answer: B

Question: 97
Which of the following is most likely to perform a direct in-place update?
A. An update that causes a varchar column to expand
B. An update that causes a varchar column to shrink
C. An update to a char column that doesnt allow null values
D. An update that changes a null value to a non-null value
Answer: C

Question: 98
Which type of partitioned table may have a clustered or non-clustered global index?
A. List
B. Hash
C. Range
D. Roundrobin
Answer: D

Question: 99
Given the following query :
SET showplan, noexec on
GO
SELECT * from authors a, titleauthor ta, titles t where ta.au_id=a.au_id and ta.title_id=t.title_id
Which statement SHOULD be appended to enable hash join?
A. plan (use optgoal allrows_dss)
B. plan (use optgoal allrows_oltp)
C. plan (use optgoal allrows_mix)
D. set optgoal allrows_mix
Answer: A

Question: 100
If a query should use Nested Loop Joins, what optimization goal setting is recommended?
A. None, use the default
B. allrows_mix
C. allrows_oltp
D. allrows_dss
Answer: C

Question: 101

Which of the following is a Non-Semantic Partitioning Strategy?
A. Range
B. Round-robin
C. Hash
D. List
Answer: B

Question: 102
QP Metrics allow a user to capture the (Choose 2)
A. Indexes chosen by the optimizer.
B. Table join order.
C. Cpu execution time.
D. Number of logical I/O used.
E. Number of rows returned.
F. Number of worktables used.
Answer: C, D

Question: 103
All tables in ASE 15 are considered to be
A. APL.
B. DOL.
C. Indexed.
D. Partitioned.
Answer: D

Question: 104
Which of the following are correct about insensitive cursors? (Choose 2)
A. The data set can become stale.
B. Locks cannot be released even after the completion of the work table.
C. Changes to the base tables are not seen by the cursor.
D. Waiting may be required to find the next row.
Answer: A, C

Question: 105
Which set option commands show the details of the join ordering algorithm? (Choose 2)
A. show_best_plan
B. show_search_engine
C. show_counters
D. show_elimination
Answer: A, B

Question: 106
What two commands are required to display the logical operators tree of a query plan in the server error log when a query is executed?
A. 'dbcc traceon(3604)' and 'set option show_lop on'
B. 'dbcc traceon(3605)' and 'set option show_lop on'
C. 'dbcc traceon(3604)' and 'set option show_best_plan'
D. 'dbcc traceon(3605)' and 'set option show_best_plan'
Answer: B

Question: 107
Which technique would NOT cause a Third Normal Form table to become denormalized?
A. inter-row derived column
B. intra-row derived column
C. duplicate column
D. merging of a subtype/supertype relationship
Answer: D

Question: 108
When designing a table, a candidate key must satisfy all of the following conditions EXCEPT
A. The key must uniquely identify the row.
B. The key must indicate the row's position in the table.
C. The key must be mandatory.
D. Each non key attribute is functionally dependent upon it.
Answer: B

Question: 109
Which database objects can a stored procedure create? (Choose 2)
A. View
B. Index
C. Default
D. Table
Answer: B, D

Question: 110
Which operation can NOT be done in a trigger?
A. Delete
B. Insert
C. Rollback
D. Truncate table
Answer: D

Question: 111
Which of the following statements are NOT true about stored procedures?
A. Stored procedures are parsed at creation time
B. Stored procedure source code can be hidden in the syscomments table
C. Stored procedures must be optimized every time they execute
D. Stored procedures query plans are stored in the procedure cache
Answer: C

Question: 112
Given the following stored procedure:
create procedure au_city_names
@pub_name varchar(30)
as
declare @city varchar(25)
select @city = city
from publishers
where pub_name = @pub_name
select au_lname
from authors
where city = @city
For which clause will the optimizer use default statistics?
A. select @city = city
B. where pub_name = @pub_name
C. select au_lname
D. where city = @city
Answer: D

Question: 113
Which of the following statements are TRUE in reference to the output of showplan display? (Choose 3)
A. Query plans describe the order of execution from a top-down perspective.

B. Query plans can be composed from over thirty different operators.
C. Query plans are upside down trees of Operators.
D. Query plans display sub-plans that are executed in parallel.
E. Query plans show the three best plans of parallel query execution.
Answer: B, C, D

Question: 114
What is the correct step order for optimization and execution?
A. Normalize, Parse, Pre-Process, Optimize, Execute
B. Parse, Normalize, Pre-Process, Optimize, Execute
C. Pre-Process, Parse, Normalize, Optimize, Execute
D. Parse, Pre-Process, Normalize, Optimize, Execute
E. Normalize, Pre-Process, Parse, Optimize, Execute
Answer: B

Question: 115
What is the default isolation level?
A. Isolation level 0 (read uncommitted)
B. Isolation level 1 (read committed)
C. Isolation level 2 (non-repeatable reads)
D. Isolation level 3 (serializable)
Answer: B

Question: 116
Readpast instructs a command to silently skip all incompatible locks
A. Without blocking, terminating or generating an error message.
B. Without blocking or terminating but will generate an error message.
C. Without blocking, but will terminate after encountering more than two incompatible locks.
D. With some limited blocking and will terminate after encountering more than two incompatible locks.
Answer: A

Question: 117
When a deadlock occurs, which transaction will be rolled back?
A. The transaction that last obtained a lock.
B. The transaction with the fewest locks held.
C. The transaction with the smaller lock size.
D. The transaction with the fewest commands.
E. The transaction with the least accumulated CPU time.
Answer: E

Question: 118
Which of the following statements is FALSE about chained mode transaction handling?
A. SELECT @@trancount will never be less than 1.
B. SELECT INTO <table> is allowed.
C. The dataserver executes an implicit begin tran for DML.
D. An explicit commit work or rollback work is required.
Answer: B

Question: 119
Which type of lock is taken out at the table level during the creation of a non-clustered index?
A. Exclusive intent
B. Exclusive
C. Update
D. Shared
Answer: D

Question: 120
Which of the following are TRUE about ASE 15 indexes? (Choose 3)
A. Clustered indexes must be global.
B. Global indexes on list partitioned tables must be nonclustered.
C. Local clustered indexes have a data and index structure for each partition.
D. Local indexes must be clustered.
E. Local nonclustered indexes have an index structure for each partition.
Answer: B, C, E

End of Document

www.ingramcontent.com/pod-product-compliance
Lightning Source LLC
Chambersburg PA
CBHW080940170526
45158CB00008B/2320